# Bye Bye Banks?

# Bye Bye Banks?

How retail banks are being
**displaced, diminished** and **disintermediated**
by tech startups and what they can do to survive.

## JAMES HAYCOCK
with
## SHANE RICHMOND

WUNDERKAMMER

First published in the United Kingdom in 2015
by Wunderkammer, an imprint of Adaptive Lab.

ISBNs
Ebook: 978-0-9932206-3-0
Paperback: 978-0-9932206-4-7

Set in Sabon and Frutiger
Infographics by Katy Jackson & Ash Patel

Adaptive Lab
91–93 Great Eastern Street
London
EC2A 3HZ

www.adaptivelab.com

# Contents

# Acknowledgements

A huge thanks to the whole Adaptive Lab team for supporting the project and giving valuable input throughout, but especially to Katy and Ash for the brilliant artwork and Emily and Daniel for patience as several deadlines slipped past.

Thanks also to Shane Richmond for collaborating on the book and Toby Mundy for encouraging me to kick the project off.

Alessandro Hatami, John V Willshire, Lee Sankey and Pritpal S Tamber – I very much appreciate you all for taking the time to give feedback, critique and direction.

Thank you to Abi for all your support and putting up with me locking myself away at weekends. Mum and Dad: thank you both for the valuable feedback.

## Contributions from experts in the industry

The thinking in this book has come together from both personal analysis and consideration, and also by speaking to some very smart people within the industry.

To support, and challenge, the argument outlined in this book we conducted one-on-one interviews with a number of senior banking executives (details below) and a survey with 110 execs at Director through to C-Suite level in well-known

Financial Services companies. The survey was conducted in January 2015 with leading research agency, ResearchNow.

In addition, a series of round-table dinners we hosted between January 2014 and the time of going to print on the topic of change and innovation in banking have also helped inform the book. These dinners were attended by senior executives from well-known FS companies and startups including, but not limited to: AirPlus, Azimo, Barclaycard, Barclays, Experian, Fiserv, GoodBank, Guevara, Lloyds, MarketInvoice, Mondo, NewDay, Osper, Squirrel, Stripe and Virgin Money. As an aside, if you're interested in finding out more about the dinners contact: events@adaptivelab.com

With respect to the one-on-one interviews, thanks to those who can be named:

**Alessandro Hatami**, Founder of Pacemakers and former Digital Payments and Innovation Director at Lloyds Banking Group

**Allan Kite**, Director of Operations Architecture, NewDay

**Anne Boden**, CEO, Starling Bank and former COO, Allied Irish Bank

**David Birch**, Director, Consult Hyperion and author of *Identity Is The New Money*

**Ian Bromwich**, Managing Director – Digital, Barclaycard

**James Barty**, Head of European Equity Strategy, Bank of America Merrill Lynch, former strategy Director, British Bankers' Association

**Lee Sankey**, former Group Design Director, Barclays

**Richard G Brown**, Executive Architect, Banking and Financial Markets, IBM and cryptocurrency advisor

**Tom Hopkins**, Product Innovation Director, Experian Consumer Services and author of *Unthinkable*

**Travers Clarke-Walker**, CMO, Fiserv International and former MD Payments and Innovation, Barclays

And thanks also to those who chose to remain anonymous (must be something to do with the title of the book!) from other well-known banks, including Credit Suisse, Barclays Wealth and Santander.

James Haycock, 2015

# About the authors

## JAMES HAYCOCK
## Managing Director – Adaptive Lab

**James Haycock** is the founder and MD of Adaptive Lab, a pioneering digital products and services agency.

At Adaptive Lab he has grown a team of impressive and inspiring problem solvers and product builders and, alongside them, works with forward-looking leaders to tackle disruptive problems at some of the world's largest corporations across sectors including finance, telco, retail and media.

Since founding Adaptive Lab in 2009, James has become a regular commentator for trade and national press including *The Sunday Times, The Guardian, Global Banking and Finance Review* and BBC Radio.

## SHANE RICHMOND

**Shane Richmond** is a technology journalist, freelance copy-writer and consultant. He spent four years as Technology Editor at *The Telegraph* and his writing has appeared in *The Independent, Stuff* and *T3*. He has written ebooks about wearable technology and the Apple iPad. His corporate clients include HP, Canon, Samsung, Intel and BT. His television and radio appearances include Sky's Jeff Randall Live, BBC Newsnight, Radio 5 Live and the World Service.

If the rate of change on the outside exceeds the rate of change on the inside, the end is near.
**JACK WELCH**

# INTRODUCTION:
# The five minute version

We need banking but we don't need banks anymore.
**BILL GATES,** 1997

It is nearly twenty years since Bill Gates predicted the demise of banking. At that time he was Chairman of Microsoft. He has since stepped down from that role and reinvented himself as a global health campaigner and philanthropist. But the banks are still here. Are we reaching the point where Gates' vision is realised? Could we see the end of banks as we know them in the next twenty years? We believe that we could, and this book explains a new scenario of how that might happen. We have kept it short – you'll be able to read it in less than two hours – but if you are really pushed for time, then here is the five minute version of our argument.

The corporate playing field has been changed irreversibly in recent years by a new generation of companies and leaders who have torn the rulebook to pieces, adopting new technology, new working practices, and serving customers whose lives are increasingly orientated around their mobile phones.

Take the example of Jan Koum. Born in the Ukraine in 1976, Jan moved to California with his mother and grandmother in the 90s, eventually taking jobs with EY and Yahoo!

In 2009, Jan founded WhatsApp, a mobile messaging application. In February 2014, WhatsApp was bought for $19bn by Facebook, a company that itself was just ten years old at the time. At the point of its acquisition WhatsApp had 450m users globally, 7m more than Vodafone had subscribers. Together these users were sending more messages than the total global volume of SMS, an industry worth $100bn. This shift in consumer behaviour hit the network operators hard. According to industry analyst Ovum* apps like WhatsApp led to a $32.5bn decline in telco revenue globally, while Ofcom identified a £300m decline in the UK.**

The speed of growth that WhatsApp realised is eye-watering, but when you hear that it had a team of just 55, your jaw also hits the floor. In five years a young, small team had built a business that was competing on a par with one of the world's biggest brands and telcos.

And it's not just the telco operators who are feeling this competitive threat. Incumbents in the media, entertainment, travel and numerous other sectors have also been feeling the pain inflicted by tech startups chipping away at their businesses – startups that are much more nimble, with smaller teams, less physical infrastructure than traditional companies, and a product that is, in essence, simply computer code.

Uber, AirBnB, Spotify and Buzzfeed have become household names, but there are many more firms that we haven't yet heard of. Research by venture capital (VC) firm Atomico identified 134 software businesses founded since 2003 that have reached a $bn valuation. TransferWise and FundingCircle are just two UK-based Financial Services startups that have achieved that scale in the last five years, demonstrating that

---

* http://www.bloomberg.com/news/articles/2014-02-21/whatsapp-shows-how-phone-carriers-lost-out-on-33-billion

** http://stakeholders.ofcom.org.uk/binaries/research/cmr/cmr14/UK_5.pdf

# Comparing WhatsApp and Vodafone

## WhatsApp
5 Years old

**Vs**

## Vodafone Group
23 Years old

**Users 450m***

**Subscribers 443m**

**55**
Employees

**92,812**
Avg employees

### Company value

**$19bn**

**$128bn**

### Value per employee

**$345.5m**

**$1.4m**

### Business models

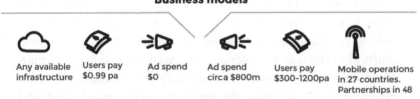

| Any available infrastructure | Users pay $0.99 pa | Ad spend $0 | Ad spend circa $800m | Users pay $300-1200pa | Mobile operations in 27 countries. Partnerships in 48 |

Data as of Feb 20th 2014 when WhatsApp was purchased by Facebook

Vodafone's value fluctuated considerably between 2014 and 2014, with the peak being $129bn in January and the lowest $83bn in October 2014

*WhatsApp active users as of 2015: 800 million

**Sources:**
Vodafone Group Annual Report 2014
http://www.vodafone.com/content/annualreport/annual_report14/downloads/full_annual_report_2014.pdf
http://ycharts.com/companies/VOD/market_cap

new entrants are already challenging the retail banking model and the established brands we all know so well.*

Like incumbents in any sector, traditional banks find it difficult to keep pace with change, due to their size and the fact that they still make considerable amounts of money. To explore new business models could cannibalise or compete with their existing one. They also find themselves hamstrung by legacy: legacy technology, legacy processes and, often, legacy thinking.

Banking giants face a further challenge, with a very high cost of compliance making it hard to deliver change at the rate of the new, agile entrants. Many in the industry feel that regulation protects them from the tech startups though. That protective cushion might be slipping away, however, as governments act to promote competition by changing regulation to encourage new entrants.

It's plain to see that a perfect storm of competition, technology, shifts in customer behaviour and regulation looks set to wreak havoc on the businesses we trust with our money, and we'll be exploring how in this book.

The book starts by outlining the significant drivers of change that impact incumbents in all sectors. The main driver is technology, which is advancing in capability and availability. This, in turn, drives two further factors: consumer behaviour, which is changing as ubiquitous connectivity and channel shifts alter the way we interact with, well, everything; and market competition – lower cost of entry means there are more competitors. In addition, the very low cost of production and distribution means these new competitors can achieve tremendous scale in no time at all.

No sector seems safe from this change. That's especially true of banking, where every aspect of the business model is being

---

* http://www.atomico.com/explore-d3

unbundled and targeted by a range of VC-backed technology companies with a very strong focus on customer experience.

Chapter Two takes the retail banking business model and highlights a small, but by no means exhaustive, list of key new entrants targeting each aspect of it. Here are a few of the areas we cover:

## Everyday banking

Thanks to regulation, this has been one of the least-contested areas of banking, despite the arrival of a few so-called "layer players" or "digital skins", such as Simple and Moven, who leverage another bank's technology and licence. However, a March 2013 change in banking regulations and authorisation processes led to a significant increase in companies looking to offer current accounts. We touch on Atom, Fidor, Good Bank, Mondo and Starling as just a few examples of companies looking to obtain a new banking license and launch within the next year to leverage the dramatically lower cost/income ratio that a branchless model offers.

## Lending

P2P lenders, now increasingly known as marketplace lenders, have attracted a lot of interest in recent years. The UK's Zopa was the first to launch, in 2005, while the SME-focused FundingCircle has recently been valued at over $1bn. In the US, Lending Club has the highest profile and IPO'd in 2014 valuing the company close to $9bn. Another type of lending, point-of-sale credit, has been offered for a long time, enticing shoppers with store cards that promise an instant discount in return for credit at, very often, high interest rates. Newcomers are seeking to disrupt this by using smart software. Affirm, for example, promises instant credit decisions on purchases based on social media data as well as traditional credit scores. Sweden's Klarna is another player in this space, claiming to have 35m customers in the ten years that it has been operating.

## Saving and investments

Digit and Acorns are two US startups helping people to save by automatically depositing into a savings account. Digit does this based on analysis of spending, while Acorns' approach is to monitor spending on any cards that have been connected to the account and round up any figure to the nearest dollar, adding the difference to the savings. While Digit doesn't currently offer any interest on its savings account (probably because they're currently not licensed to do so) Acorns offers an investment account. Other startups with a focus on investments are the UK's Nutmeg, and Betterment and Wealthfront in the US. All lower the barrier to entry for investors, offering more transparent pricing and simple, online portfolio construction and management tools supported by a digital operating model they hope will allow them to pass better returns to their customers than the alternative of a traditional wealth manager.

## Payments

The payments market is a hotly contested area, particularly around digital wallets and P2P payments. PayPal, which massively simplified the online payments process, has been freshly spun out of eBay, so is sure to pick up the pace of innovation. And of course the tech giant that many fear, Apple, has launched Apple Pay, which aims to do a similar thing but with in-store payments using an iPhone or the recently released Apple Watch. In the P2P space, companies such as Venmo are proving vastly attractive to the under-thirties, a generation that is mobile native and sees little need for banks.

## International money transfer

Transferring money overseas has long been expensive, and slower than it could be. Companies like TransferWise, which was valued at $1bn in a recent investment round, are arriving and are looking to improve on the norm. They cleverly aggregate and redirect the money going through their system so that they can transfer cash without actually sending money across borders. Azimo and WorldRemit are two similar, UK-based startups. WorldRemit says 90% of its payments are received instantly, compared with the days a payment might take using traditional transfer services.

## Money management

Personal Finance Managers (PFM) help consumers to manage their money by collecting all their financial data into a single website or app. US-based Mint was one of the first. It was founded in 2006 and was acquired by accounting software firm Intuit in 2009 for $170m. LevelMoney, started in 2012, targets Millennials who have student loans to pay back and also want to start saving.

## Money

Finally, there is disruption of money itself. The rise of Bitcoin and other virtual currencies, built on a cryptographic system called the blockchain, could radically alter the way that financial transactions are carried out. The cryptography behind the blockchain means that transactions can be verified without the need for a trusted third party – a role typically played by a bank. While these technologies are in their infancy at the moment, they are being seen as the foundation for a change as profound as the Internet itself.

In Chapter three, having given a broad overview of the new entrants in banking and the aspect of the banking model they're attacking, we outline a scenario that we believe is already well under way. We start by introducing it using the example of the telco sector and how the traditional players are being challenged in that industry, before applying it to banking. The scenario proposes that incumbents are becoming displaced, diminished and disintermediated by software businesses and new technologies.

**Displaced** – by a superior customer experience and price offered by new entrants, enabled partly by the luxury of being free of legacy technology and cost base, and teams closer to the needs of their target customers.

**Diminished** – as their business model is squeezed and they're relegated to utilities in a market with higher switching frequency. We believe this will be spurred on by the revised Directive for Payments Services (PSD2), which will require banks to offer Open APIs (Application Programming Interfaces – we'll explain what these are in the book).

**Disintermediated** – as a new technology challenges the core competency of the incumbents, which the arrival of the blockchain, an innovation still not fully understood by many, suggests it might do.

It would be naive of us to ignore the fact that there are many very smart individuals in banks who are clearly aware of the changes that are coming. To ensure a balanced perspective, we spoke to a number of senior banking executives through face-to-face interviews, a survey and a series of round-table dinners. The insight gathered through this has been used to explore, further and challenge our position. You'll find comments interspersed throughout the book sharing their view of the impact of the tech startups, the cost of compliance that the existing players are burdened with, and the contention that customers won't trust a startup with their money, as well as the blockers for innovation, for example: how can you expect an MD with P&L ownership to disrupt her business? In these conversations a theme emerged around three particular topics – people, culture and technology, which we focus on in Chapter four.

In the final chapter we briefly outline the various options that the banks are already pursuing: digital transformations, service and product innovation, and partnering or investing with startups. While we believe these can deliver change, our opinion is that they'll struggle to impact on those three critical components of an organisation highlighted as a challenge in the interviews: its people, culture and its technology. With that in mind, we outline what we believe to be the answer: the Beta Bank.

A Beta Bank is a standalone organisation with a separate leadership and HQ. A fresh start, offering the opportunity to rethink from the ground up. We outline a ten point operating model for banking leaders to consider. We believe this approach is the best opportunity for a bank to design a proposition, servicing model and, critically, an organisation built for a future where the pace of change is only set to increase, not an adapted version of a business model that hasn't changed in hundreds of years.

That is a summary of our position, and you will find more detail in the following pages. The scale of this coming change should not be underestimated, and it has not gone unnoticed by banking leaders. Neelie Kroes, Head of the European Commission's Digital Agenda, said at Davos in 2014: "I've met with bank CEOs who tell me all their business models are about to be torn to shreds, that the future is mostly virtual banking and their main competitors are tech companies not other banks."

Speaking at Davos a year later, the Bank of England Governor, Mark Carney, stated that the banking sector was vulnerable to an Uber-type incursion and that such a situation was imminent.

The forces driving this change are undeniable. It is a matter of when, not if, banking is reinvented.

# 1. THE FORCES OF DESTRUCTION:
## Change and what drives it

In 1871, Finnish mining engineer, Fredrik Idestam, had two paper mills in south-western Finland. He decided his company needed a new name, and settled on Nokia, after the town closest to one of his mills. Fastforward almost a century to 1967 and Idestam's Nokia Ab merged with Finnish Rubber Works – founded in 1898 – and Finnish Cable Works Ltd, a company formed in 1912, to form the Nokia Corporation. The new Nokia had five core businesses: rubber, cable, forestry, electronics and power generation.

Some years later, in 1989, Nokia produced its first mobile phone, beginning a switch to telecoms. By 1998 it was the world's largest mobile phone manufacturer, and turnover had reached €31bn. In nine years the company went from market entry to market dominance. However, an event just another nine years later dented that dominance irreversibly.

The 2007 launch of Apple's iPhone wrong-footed Nokia, which couldn't produce a smartphone with similar consumer appeal. Nokia's dominance in feature phones – the low-end handsets lacking the advanced functionality of smartphones – meant that it remained the world's largest mobile phone manufacturer until 2012, but the decline had begun long before. In September 2013, following second quarter losses of €115m, Nokia sold its mobile phone business to Microsoft for $7bn, a fraction of its turnover, let alone its market value, in 1998.

Working against Nokia, and all businesses, is a force known as "creative destruction". It is not a new concept; in fact, it derives from Karl Marx. In essence, it says that the economy is always undergoing revolution – its structure, and the companies within it, under attack from and being rebuilt by new processes, markets and developments. Nokia had successfully transitioned between business models on a number of occasions, something that many businesses struggle with, but the transition to smartphones was one too many.

Furthermore, the rate of creative destruction is increasing and, as a result, company lifespans are getting shorter. Research by Yale's Professor Richard Foster demonstrates that corporations in the Standard and Poor 500 in 1958 spent an average of 61 years on the list. That had fallen to 25 years by 1980, and to just 18 years by 2012.*

In 2012, Chris Zook, a partner at Bain and Company, said: "We have never seen companies losing their leadership positions as quickly as they are today. A list of the top 20 banks today contains only seven that were on the list a decade ago. A similar pattern holds for airlines. And for telecom. And for many others."**

We believe that this increasing pace of change is being driven by three significant, and linked, forces: technology, shifting consumer behaviour and increasing competition. In this chapter we will explain these forces, and look at some examples of the impact they've had.

---

* http://www.innosight.com/innovation-resources/strategy-innovation/creative-destruction-whips-through-corporate-america.cfm
** https://hbr.org/2012/06/when-creative-destruction-dest

## 1.1 The Forces of change

Of these three forces of change, advancing technology is the most significant because it enables and fuels the others. New, more powerful technology has arrived and, with ever lower costs, access to it has grown considerably. The always-on, always-connected nature of this technology has driven shifts in consumer behaviour, and transformed the competitive land-scape of sectors as diverse as retail and healthcare.

The first personal computer, Olivetti's Programma 101, was launched in 1965 at a price of $3,200. It wasn't until the early 1990s, however, that the PC became a presence in the average home. Fastforward to September 2014, and the latest iPhone contains 625 times more transistors than a 1995 Intel Pentium-powered PC, at around a quarter of the price. The launch week-end of the last iPhone saw Apple sell twenty-five times more CPU transistors than were in all the PCs on Earth in 1995.

The Internet, connecting all these devices to the world's information, arrived in British homes in the early 1990s, at a speed of around 64 kilobits-per-second (Kbps). Anyone who used it at that time will remember the wait while the modem dialled-in to the network and the slow loading times for web-sites as text and pictures slipped into place a bit at a time. These days, most British homes have sufficient Internet speed to stream live video – something that requires a connection of 8–10 megabits-per-second (Mbps). Once you understand that a megabit is 1,000 kilobits, you can begin to understand just how much faster Internet speeds have become in twenty years. The current fastest Internet connections available in UK homes offer more than 150Mbps.

Meanwhile, mobile broadband speeds have also been steadily climbing. The 2G Internet speeds – up to 237Kbps – that first brought the mobile Internet to a mainstream audience soon increased to an average of 6.1Mbps on 3G in the UK, and are increasing to around 15Mbps as 4G rolls out across the country.

Not only has consumer technology and speed of connectivity changed but the tools used to create services and applications have also drastically changed. The arrival of open source technologies brought software that was powerful and freely available to anyone. First becoming popular in the late 1990s, open source made a significant impact in a couple of ways, both relating to cost. Firstly, and most obviously, the lack of software licensing fees lowered development costs. Secondly, the inherent sharing of work that happens in open source communities means a business building software today doesn't have to design and produce code for every feature of their application, meaning the commodity functionality can be quickly integrated. A user login model will already be available, a powerful search engine technology could easily be integrated with via an API, a library that manages easy scanning of an uploaded document through optical character recognition will be available off the shelf.

The emergence of cloud technology, a term popularised in 2006 by Amazon with their launch of Elastic Compute Cloud, Platform-as-a-Service and Infrastructure-as-a-Service had a further impact on cost and enabled companies adopting it to scale quickly and cost-efficiently. These services provide access to vital components for running a company, but only as-and-when the company needs them. Instead of, for example, predicting when you will need a new server, ordering it, configuring it and turning it on, companies can just rent more server capacity from a cloud provider. Likewise, powerful scaling, monitoring and load balancing technology, which would previously have had to be designed and coded by each business, is now available for rent as part of a packaged service from companies such as Heroku and Amazon Web Services. And not only is a rental model preferable, but the costs of rental are also decreasing significantly.

Marc Andreessen, co-founder of Netscape, the first Internet browser, and now a partner in prominent Silicon Valley VC, Andreessen Horowitz, said: "In 2000, when my partner Ben Horowitz was CEO of the first cloud computing company, Loudcloud, the cost of a customer running a basic Internet application was approximately $150,000 a month. Running that same application today in Amazon's cloud costs about $1,500 a month."

Lower startup costs, increased availability of cheap capital (increasingly so with the growth of crowdfunding services) and easy access to global audiences through cheap media, Google and the App Store have combined to create an opportunity for a new category of company – the software company. These companies can challenge established players without major infrastructure or staffing costs.

"Software," Andreessen argues, "is eating the world". The table on page 16 shows just a few examples of these companies, and the businesses they are challenging.

These advances in technology, combined with increasing access to it and a range of new businesses, have driven considerable changes in consumer behaviour over the last 20 years. In 1995, according to World Bank figures, just 2% of Britons were online. By 1999 it was more than 20%, and in 2013 UK Internet penetration was 89.8%. Mobile use has grown even faster. Ofcom reported that by Q1 2014 93% of adults in the UK owned a mobile phone and 61% of the population owned a smartphone, giving them access to a powerful computer and, through it, access to the world's information.*

This access has transformed every sector and business you can think of. The high street has been decimated, and many previously massive brands, such as Woolworths and Comet,

---

* http://data.worldbank.org/indicator/IT.NET.USER.P2?page=3

# Startup disruptors

| New entrant | Disrupting | How |
|---|---|---|
| Uber | Traditional taxi cabs | Uber owns no cars; it simply uses an innovative software model to connect freelance drivers with users who need a ride. |
| AirBnB | Hotel industry | AirBnB is the biggest hotel brand in the world. It's a platform that connects people with spare rooms with people looking for an interesting place to stay and takes a fee on the transaction, all without owning any real estate. |
| WhatsApp | Telco companies/ SMS | Whatsapp provides a cheaper but more feature-rich, cross-platform MMS experience. |
| Skype | Telco companies/ international roaming | Skype offers a free way to speak to people around the world on video. |
| Spotify | Traditional music industry | Spotify offers unlimited music on demand for a monthly subscription (or the cost of a single CD). |
| Netflix | Movie rental shops and cableTV | Netflix provides a platform via the Internet to watch the latest movies and series, as well as their own exclusive series for a smaller fee than cable networks and rental shops. |

have gone, due to the ease, wide selection and often lower prices available online.

The Internet has also made it easier for consumers to research purchases. Customer reviews inform purchase decisions on products ranging from kettles and TVs to holidays and cars. Likewise, the Internet has broken down borders, making it simple to order products from other countries

This change in consumer behaviour has forced companies to change how they do business. Pre-Internet, the options for selling to customers were simple: mail order, shops or door-to-door sales staff. All were expensive in different ways, which created a high barrier to entry. After the Internet, any business with a website could compete – at vastly less cost – allowing them, especially in the case of Amazon, to compete aggressively.

In Amazon's wake came other online-only success stories, such as ASOS, which launched in 2000 and by 2013 had revenues of £753m. Online-only retailers have reshaped numerous verticals, from travel (Expedia) to DIY (Screwfix).

As consumers moved to smartphones, they started to use them for online shopping as well. But smartphones are capable of much more than simply browsing the web. Add mobile apps and your "phone" is not just a personal communications tool but a media storage device, compact camera, fitness tracker, navigation aid, activist toolkit, games console and all manner of other things besides. Many of the apps being offered by software companies challenge well-known and established companies.

The true, transformative impact of the smartphone has still not been fully realised. Between now and 2020, another billion people will come online, most of them on smartphones, according to the International Telecommunications Union, meaning that 80% of the world's adults will have access to these powerful, connected devices.

This triangulation of connectivity, technology and software has culminated in services like Uber, which is disrupting the

# Competing on customer experience

Startups compete with incumbents by improving customer experience.

## Uber vs traditional taxis

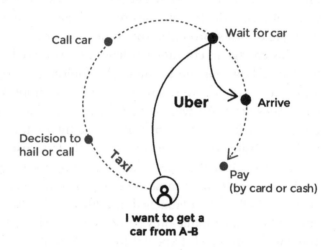

Call car

Wait for car

Uber

Arrive

Decision to hail or call

Taxi

Pay
(by card or cash)

I want to get a
car from A-B

## Amazon vs book strores

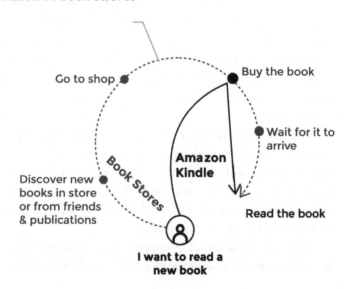

Go to shop

Buy the book

Wait for it to arrive

Amazon
Kindle

Book Stores

Discover new
books in store
or from friends
& publications

Read the book

I want to read a
new book

taxi business across the world. Despite being the largest taxi company in the world Uber has no taxis. The lack of overheads – in cab office staff and dispatchers, and the more efficient use of driver time – less time wasted driving around in search of a fare, and a quicker and cheaper service for the passenger are the main reasons why Uber – and services like it – are currently growing so quickly. Uber didn't need to build its own payment and mapping technologies – the App Store takes care of distribution and marketing to a large degree and the company has not had to spend much on marketing in each new city. Uber's success is entirely powered by the forces described earlier.

But Uber is not unusual. It is one of many software businesses taking on established sectors, including banking. The new entrants to banking are many and they are attacking different parts of the business. Could one of them be the Uber of banking?

# 2. UNBUNDLING THE BANKS:
# Startups and the bit of the banking model they're after

Banking has suffered a significant amount of turbulence over the last few years but little of it has been due to creative destruction. And yet only seven of today's top 20 US banks were in the top 20 a decade ago. The increasingly rapid turnover of companies at the top of their industry is already affecting banking, and they seem set for further turbulence, this time driven by new customer behaviours and by the arrival of new competitors.

> The advent of mobile in the last few years has really changed the way people behave. Close to 15 million banking apps have now been downloaded and across them there are 7 million daily logins. The speed of this has been enormous. Meanwhile, footfall in some branches is down 30% in a similar time period.
>
> Anonymous banking executive

As with incumbents in all sectors, banks have struggled with this shift to digital and to meet the customers' experience expectations. *

Despite the impact the Internet has had on sales and distribution in other sectors, the retail banking model is only recently starting to leverage this opportunity.

> Some places, you can apply for a credit card or savings account online. It takes the pain out of the process. Think about a mortgage application. You're going to want to be able to do the vast majority of that online rather than having to spend four hours on the phone with a mortgage adviser.
>
> Anonymous banking executive

Once logged in, most banks present their customers with a user experience that has not changed much from the web of 2000, centred on a basic online view of a printed statement. Commonsense interactions such as, for example, a search function for your bank statements or the option to sort transactions by date or amount, are not possible on many bank websites. The banks' mobile apps, while starting to improve, suffer from a similar lack of functionality, offering even less than the websites – most banks will let you pay someone only if they are on your payments list.

However, every limit on functionality, every obstacle in the user experience, might be an opportunity for a new entrant.

---

* Inability to quickly react to changing consumer needs was highlighted as a key challenge in our survey. Perhaps because they're not engaging with end users as best they could – 61% don't believe retail banks could improve this. Adaptive Lab / Research Now banking industry quantitative research study – Jan 2015.

While a few of these entrants are setting out to offer a full, digital banking proposition, most are unbundling the traditional business model.

> What we are thinking is going to happen is that the model is going to disintegrate. The banks won't be able to control it all forever. As well as challenger banks, you're going to have challenger models.
>
> **ANNE BODEN,** CEO, Starling Bank

Unbundling is a crucial point in digital disruption for many sectors, but especially in banking. Banks leverage their current account relationship to offer savings, and lending through overdrafts, credit cards, loans and mortgages. But each of these products is in effect a separate business with separate teams, priorities, technology, experience and, of course, legacy. The banks are struggling with a legacy of decades of these products delivered to many customer segments, across many channels in many territories, and the inflexible technology infrastructure that comes with this complication.

> You've got myriad systems and processes which have been joined up over multiple layers. Imagine the situation, you've got lots and lots of customer segments. Then you've got lots and lots of channels. Then you've got lots and lots of products . . . Then you link them all together by putting lots and lots of layers over them. That's just so difficult. The first thing you have to do is make sure you keep up with all the regulatory change. Then you have to try and think about how you're going to give the customer a great experience.
>
> **ANNE BODEN,** CEO, Starling Bank

In contrast, however, many of the new entrants focus on a single aspect of the banking model and, because of this focus, and because of the luxury of having no legacy, are able to excel in offering a superior experience.

As one might imagine, given the size of the markets they're taking on, the startups looking to improve on this are attracting increasing sums of money with venture capitalists pouring money into the financial technology or fintech sector. CB Insights reports that global investment in fintech grew from around $1bn in 2008 to over $12bn in 2014. Despite this growth of interest from investors, our survey revealed that awareness within the banking industry of these new entrants isn't as high as one might expect (see table opposite).

So who are these startups, and what is it that they're doing? In the following section we will highlight just a few new companies tackling various aspects of the banking model, including everyday banking, lending, savings and investments, payments, international money transfer, money management and money itself.

## 2.1 Everyday banking

Current accounts are the central point of people's financial lives. It's the place their salary is paid into and the point from which they access their money on a day-to-day basis.

Traditionally delivered through a branch network, the arrival of the Internet created opportunities to acquire and service customers through online channels and realise the cost savings of doing so.

The idea of an Internet-only bank looking to leverage this opportunity isn't new. The late 90s saw several Internet banks launch, such as Cooperative Bank's Smile and HSBC's First Direct, which expanded from telephone banking into online.

Much has changed since the 1990s though and, with the

# Awareness of startups in executive at banks

We asked 110 senior execs ranging from director to C-suite about the startups they were aware of.

| Entrants | I'm aware of the company and what they do | I'm aware of them but don't know what they do | I've never heard of them |
|---|---|---|---|
| nutmeg | 23% | 35% | 43% |
| Betterment | 8% | 19% | 73% |
| Square | 15% | 27% | 57% |
| venmo | 6% | 15% | 78% |
| azimo | 6% | 26% | 67% |
| TransferWise | 15% | 35% | 51% |
| LendingClub | 18% | 36% | 45% |
| Rate%Setter | 17% | 26% | 56% |
| PayPal | 92% | 8% | 0% |

Adaptive Lab / Research Now banking industry quantitative research study – Jan 2015

transformational impact of the Internet accelerating, consumers increasingly familiar with interacting online, and their expectations set by the likes of Apple, Google and Facebook, the time is right for the digital challengers to make a broader impact than those early digital banking models.

While the timing seems right, one of the challenges for new entrants targeting this aspect of the banking model is the regulatory barrier. Some have looked to work around this hurdle by creating a "layer player" or "digital skin", building a modern customer experience and proposition but sitting on top of another bank's core banking system and licence.

Simple, which launched in the US in 2012, is one example of a company that took this approach and was lauded for its digital experience when it launched, with reports of people queuing at its virtual door during its private beta stage, during which access was invite-only.

Their website looks much more like that of a tech company, promoting and demonstrating their account features and emphasising the quality of its customer service with pictures of their support team.

The features offered by the bank include smart budgeting tools seldom offered by traditional banks. Safe-to-Spend is one example. It betters a traditional account balance by taking into consideration forthcoming payments, and other regular activities, so that the customer doesn't have to remember to factor them in when calculating how much money is available to spend right now.

Another feature that it offers is savings goals, which, on the surface, seem like the functionality found in typical PFMs, but in the case of Simple it automatically adds money towards those goals, with the amounts taken into consideration in the Safe-to-Spend amount.

Their search feature is also much more powerful than that found in most interfaces offered by a traditional bank, if indeed transaction search is even offered. Simple allows customers to search for "weekday lunch" or "dinner over 30 in Portland", which is better than poring over hard-to-read transactions or even having to download a pdf or csv file to search manually.

While Simple made waves with its launch, and other similar propositions, like Moven for example, have also launched, none have made a significant change to the shape of the market. However, that might not be the case for much longer, following a recent regulatory change in the UK.

In March 2013 the Financial Services Authority (FSA) conducted a review to consider how to reduce the barrier to entry. Following the review, the Prudential Regulation Authority and the Financial Conduct Authority – the two bodies that replaced the FSA in April 2013 – implemented changes to banking regulation and the authorisation process intended to make it easier for companies to apply for a banking licence. The change has had the intended result, with twenty-nine firms applying for a banking licence in 2014, and a number of new banks seem set to launch in the UK in 2015 and 2016, some of whom are focusing on a digital banking proposition.*

One of the new banks is Atom. The business was founded by Anthony Thomson, who previously launched Metro Bank, and will be run by Mark Mullen, who was previously CEO of one of the UK's other innovative banking entrants – First Direct.

The company will be based in Durham and, by leveraging its leaner, digital-only operating model, will look to offer better savings and loan rates than rivals, according to Thomson.**

Paul Lamacraft, fund manager at Woodford Investment Management, one of Atom's investors, told the *Guardian* news-

---

* http://www.thisismoney.co.uk/money/saving/article-2606119/FCA-reveals-29-firms-lodged-banking-licence-applications.html

** http://www.thisismoney.co.uk/money/saving/article-2906596/Atom-Bank-founder-promises-competitive-savings-rates-current-accounts-opens-virtual-doors-later-year.html

paper: "With no branch network, an outsourced infrastructure and no legacy issues, Atom bank's running costs should be significantly lower than the competition."*

Other UK digital banking startups include Starling, Mondo and Good Bank. Starling, previously known as Bank Possible, was founded by Anne Boden, formerly COO of Allied Irish Banks. Mondo, founded by Tom Blomfield, who previously co-founded the innovative payments startup GoCardless, and Jason Bates, has ambitious plans to create a "full stack bank", building their infrastructure from the ground up, which they believe is key to enabling them to deliver the real time experience that customers expect. Good Bank is also founded by a seasoned fintech entrepreneur. Ricky Knox previously founded Small World Financial Services, a successful money transfer business, and followed that with another money transfer startup – Azimo.

At the time of writing, Atom, Good Bank, Mondo and Starling hadn't given a lot away about what they will offer, other than saying that mobile will be a key focus and that they're likely to have a full service offering from a financial services product perspective (or present one through partners) albeit not necessarily from launch. Whether they'll have the types of features and functionality that Simple offers is unknown but it can be assumed that they will. The features offered by another digital banking startup are clearer to see, however.

Fidor, a German bank, launched in 2007. Originally just operating in Germany, it later expanded into Russia and has plans to launch in the UK this year, once it has been permitted access to the payment networks.

Fidor offers a multi-currency digital wallet, incentivises customers to like it on Facebook in return for improved interest

---

* http://www.theguardian.com/business/2014/dec/04/neil-woodford-fund-manager-invests-online-only-internet-bank-atom

rates, and it also takes a novel approach to customer support by paying customers to help with support queries.

The business also offers Open APIs. This approach likens the bank to such companies as Facebook and Twitter who have, through offering access to their data and services, enabled third-party companies to create applications on top of their platform to better serve the needs of their customer base as well as drive revenue. It's too early to tell how Fidor's API programme is performing but this thinking demonstrates that they're planning to take a more innovative approach than the traditional players: only 35% of the Senior Banking Executives we surveyed thought the use of APIs was a good idea.*

A further example of Fidor's innovative approach can be seen in a service they launched that allows its customers to instantly trade Bitcoins through a partnership with German Bitcoin exchange bictoin.de, overcoming the delay that users of the exchange typically have. Further demonstration of their open approach to partnering with cryptocurrency businesses is that they were the first bank to integrate with Ripple, a payment protocol similar in concept to the blockchain, which allows Fidor customers to transfer money internationally at no cost.

Despite innovative features that Fidor and the other digital challengers will offer, capturing enough market share to build a viable business is going to be hard. Leaked data** suggests that Simple has struggled to acquire customers, which is potentially why they went down the route of an acquisition with BBVA Compass. Likewise, Moven's recent partnership announcement with Accenture, in which their technology will be sold through

---

* Adaptive Lab / Research Now banking industry quantitative research study – Jan 2015

** http://qz.com/213192/banking-startup-simple-seems-to-be-struggling-to-sign-up-active-users/

the consultancy, might suggest that they've also struggled to realise growth with a B2C model.*

One reason that we haven't seen a digital challenger demonstrate significant growth might simply be that the perceived benefits don't outweigh the hassle of switching.

> Most people do not switch bank accounts. That's because they struggle to identify a problem. If moving is a hassle, and there's no problem to solve, then it's all just unnecessary risk and effort.
> **TOM HOPKINS**, Product Innovation Director, Experian Consumer Services

Trust is also likely to be a considerable factor as to whether consumers will deposit money with the new entrants, and is a factor that arose in all of our interviews with senior banking executives.

> Customer trust is something that isn't built overnight; it takes years and years to build. Unless these new banks are able to prove that they will be around for the long term, as a consumer, I would be concerned about having my savings or the money that I earned be stored with them.
> **ALESSANDRO HATAMI**, former Lloyds executive

Many of the above-mentioned companies are targeting millennials or even, more broadly, those with a millennial mindset. This group already bank though, so the question is – do they think their current bank is good enough, or might they be prepared to switch?

---

* https://newsroom.accenture.com/industries/banking/accenture-and-moven-join-forces-to-transform-digital-banking-solutions.htm

When speaking to millenials it's common to hear that they bank with the company their parents did, which highlights the importance there has been to date of capturing those first entering the market. In the UK there are two startups targeting this younger segment: Osper and GoHenry. Both, further examples of layer players, they offer pre-paid debit cards for children but offer the parental controls to help appeal to parents acting as a route to market.

Regardless of the demographic targeted though, how is it that these new entrants are going to differentiate? A good digital experience, given that all the major players are making significant improvements, is unlikely to be enough. It will have to be a truly differentiated proposition as well.

> I think new entrants need to differentiate by providing a very different customer proposition and experience. Doing the same as an existing bank doesn't really work. People are not switching banks at present as they don't see anything different in the marketplace. There has to be something really different in order to attract the customers.
>
> **ANNE BODEN**, CEO, Starling Bank

And, proposition aside, a critical question that came up frequently in our interviews is whether the new banks will be able to reach the scale required to make the traditional retail banking business model work.

> If they can scale quickly enough, before they burn through their cash, and be competitive, they have a chance. They obviously don't have to get to the same scale because their overheads are lower. But there is a minimum scale they need to get to in order to be competitive enough to

compete with the rest of the banks. I don't know if it's
even about the technology. I think it's almost a marketing
play. Can they identify their customers fast enough to
get the deposits in quickly enough, and be able to deploy
the money back out again prudently enough, with a high
enough return, that they can get to a rate where they get
past that inflection point and start to really grow?

Anonymous banking executive

Of course, these comments assume that the new entrants will
adopt the same business model. Data and the opportunities
related to this, despite still being unproven at scale in banking,
might present an alternative or additional revenue stream, and
came up on a number of occasions in speaking to our inter-
viewees.

Banks and financial institutions are realising that there's
a lot of information on the customer that is built into the
data generated by their transacting with the bank. This
information has value, and it can generate a relationship,
a tighter relationship with the customer that currently
the banks are not benefiting from.

Anonymous banking executive

While this category of startup will bring some much needed
competition into the market, our opinion is that to succeed
they will need to be more focussed in their customer segment
than millenials, being a truly differentiated proposition, fault-
less experience, excellence at customer acquisition and on-
boarding, all while being able to build trust quickly and backed
by a lean operating model and smart business model.

## 2.2 Lending

> Banks earned about $150 billion in 2014, and we
> estimate $11 billion plus, or 7% of annual profit, could
> be at risk from these new sources of credit over the next
> five-plus years.
>
> Goldman Sachs research*

Lending, whether it be through overdrafts, loans, mortgages or credit cards, is where the banks make a significant proportion of their revenue, and for that reason make it an area of considerable interest to new entrants.

Peer-to-peer (P2P) lending is one example of an alternative lending model that has grown significantly in recent years. Unlike personal loans offered by banks, capital for loans offered through P2P isn't provided by the company but instead, as the name suggests, from other people. As such, the P2P companies act as market makers, connecting groups of individuals to each other to facilitate a loan.

> I think P2P is here to stay, and I think it will grow. It
> won't replace all lending, but it definitely has a niche.
>
> **ALESSANDRO HATAMI**, former Lloyds executive

The UK's Zopa was the first P2P lender, launching in 2005. Prosper and Lending Club were among the first to launch in the US, in 2006 and 2007 respectively, but since then there has been a wave of further entrants.

While at first the US platforms didn't perform well for

---

* http://www.bloomberg.com/news/articles/2015-03-04/shadow-banks-could-take-11-billion-annual-profit-goldman-says

investors, with 40% of loans defaulting on Prosper and 24% at Lending Club, their performance has improved significantly, largely through better credit-risk profiling, which they now identify as one of their core strengths.

These companies have grown at great speed, with Lending Club's IPO in late December valuing the company at $8.5bn. Despite this rapid growth, they are barely scratching the surface of the addressable market. According to their website, Lending Club facilitated over $1.4bn in loans in the last quarter of 2014, doubling from the same quarter of 2013. As context, industry experts say the market for personal debt is worth $3 trillion in the US.

Lending Club says it aims to transform the banking system by making credit more affordable and investing more rewarding. Its rapid growth was probably driven by a combination of factors: first, a reduction in the availability of loans from traditional institutions during the financial crisis; second, the rates offered for investors and borrowers by the P2P platforms are often preferable; and finally, by creating a new investment opportunity for average investors.

So how do the rates compare? As of January 2014, Lending Club's website reported historical returns of grade A-C borrowers (their credit score) of between 4.74% and 7.98%, rates that are attracting the attention of more investors.

> While I haven't seen large-scale money move, clients are certainly talking about [P2P] and are starting to invest.
> Anonymous banking executive

These preferential rates are possible because of, as Lending Club states in their IPO filing, their "innovative marketplace model that efficiently connects the supply and demand of capital; online operations that substantially reduce the need

for physical infrastructure and improve convenience; and automation that increases efficiency, reduces manual processes and
improves borrower and investor experience".

To support this, research by McKinsey and Librium outlined that Lending Club's operating costs were at 2.70% of
their outstanding loan volume while banks' costs were 6.95%,
with the costs of the branch network making up over 2%.*

And it's not just personal loans that are being offered, with
Lending Club and many others starting to branch out. Lending
Club is already lending to small businesses through a deal with
Google, one of its investors, and more recently announced a
similar deal in the US with Alibaba, the Chinese e-commerce
giant. Google plans to offer loans of up to $600,000 through
the marketplace to their Google for Work partners who
number some 10,000. Alibaba, meanwhile, has millions of
small business customers who might be eligible for financing.
These examples of supplier financing are just one new form
of product Lending Club is offering. Through an acquisition
of Springstone Financial they are also offering medical and
educational loans. In the future, Renaud Laplanche, the Chief
Executive, says the company also plans to offer credit cards,
mortgages and more.

As well as expansion in their product offering, the P2P
platforms have also been expanding the sources of capital, to
include money from institutional investors, and in doing so are
increasingly referring to themselves as marketplace lenders. An
example of this in the UK is the recent partnership between
Zopa and Metro Bank.**

This activity is accelerating so much in the US that the more

---

* http://www.slideshare.net/seanbash/renaud-laplanchelendingclublend-it2014key
note (slide 25)

** http://www.ft.com/cms/s/0/efadf6fc-fd67-11e4-9e96-00144feabdc0.html#axzz3b3
Pg EX9m

advanced needs of this aspect of the supply side of the market are being met by the P2P platforms offering API access to their marketplaces. This allows investors to programmatically build and manage loan portfolios. A further demonstration in the growth of this activity is the launch of Orchard, which acts as a secondary marketplace that aggregates loans from across the platforms.

While this provides much higher volumes of capital for lending which is good for the borrower side, this development is being criticised by some as it crowds out the average investor making it harder for them to access the best opportunities.

This criticism aside, the marketplace lending sector is growing increasingly competitive. Lending Club is far from being alone in the P2P market. In the UK, Zopa and Rate-Setter are offering personal loans, while Auxmoney are doing it in Germany. Zopa, FundingCircle (who were valued at $1bn in a recent fundraising round), MoneyandCo are serving the requirements of small businesses here in the UK, while On-Deck is doing so in the US. Mortgages are being offered by LendingHome in the US, while SoFi helps students repay their debt.*

As well as becoming increasingly crowded, P2P lending is also receiving considerable political support. Two changes instigated by the government look set to drive further growth. Firstly a new ISA targeted at P2P investing is being discussed. and secondly George Osborne recently announced that the first £1,000 invested through P2P sites would be tax free. Further political support has been shown to encourage small business lending through the platforms.**

Vince Cable, the former Business Secretary, said in a *Finan-*

---

* http://www.ft.com/cms/s/0/a10fce2a-e832-11e4-894a-00144feab7de.html

** http://www.telegraph.co.uk/finance/personalfinance/savings/11489834/First-1000-of-peer-to-peer-returns-will-be-tax-free.html

*cial Times* article: "Too much business lending is concentrated in the big banks. If we're to have a properly functioning business lending market, they need to be challenged by new banks, peer-to-peer lenders and other alternative providers."

George Osborne, the Chancellor of the Exchequer, has said that British banks will be required to refer rejected loan applications from SMEs to P2P platforms for financing. RBS and Santander are the first to be doing so.

Finally the government's British Business Bank has invested £200m through seven P2P platforms including FundingCircle, MarketInvoice, RateSetter and Zopa, to stimulate small business growth.

Despite the progress these entrants are making and the support they are receiving from the government, they interestingly don't appear to be seen as a credible threat by the Senior Banking Executives we surveyed.\* 45% hadn't even heard of Lending Club while 36% knew the brand, but didn't know what it is that they do. For Ratesetter it was 56% and 26%.

Despite the banking industry seeming not to have the P2P brands on their radar, it isn't the only new lending model they should be keeping a watch for. Another, although one not receiving the same level of interest, is point-of-sale credit.

Affirm is one of the startups gathering momentum in this area. Its founder Max Levchin, who previously founded PayPal, says that with PayPal "we stopped short of changing the system" but, Affirm, he says his goal is to "reimagine the idea of a bank from the ground up".

Affirm's first product, Split Pay, offers consumers a loan at the point of purchase, alongside options to pay by card, both facilitated through an online payment form designed to work well on mobile.

---

\* Adaptive Lab / Research Now banking industry quantitative research study – Jan 2015

Affirm allows customers to split their payment for a purchase over a three- six- or twelve-month period. It offers a real-time decision on the loan application, and does so by employing a vast array – around 70,000 – of personal qualities, including social media data as well as traditional credit scores. They claim to offer a richer picture of the borrower's financial profile than the traditional credit scores, which makes them a better option for segments known for having a thin credit file, such as students and those in the armed services.

Affirm, which will make money through interest on loans and as a payment processor, was originally funded by Levchin himself, but more recently raised $45m. It offers rates that range from 10–30%, which are broadly comparable to credit cards, but it intends to both be proactive about communicating upcoming payments and to focus on transparency and fairness, with no late fees and interest that doesn't compound. Targeting millennials, who Levchin says have "absolutely no love for banks", the company is focused on mobile payments and makes it very easy for merchants to integrate its payment technology. Like many modern companies, Affirm plans to distribute itself through an API.

Levchin's former company PayPal also offers consumers a line of credit at point of purchase and, like Affirm, claims a superior risk model with the ability to offer instant decisions. PayPal Credit, as the service is known, follows the acquisition of a company called Bill Me Later. A fast and simple application process at the point of sale that saves form-filling and having to wait for a response is the experience advantage; however, its model doesn't offer the same transparency or fairness as Affirm with late fees.

Sweden's Klarna is another player in this space, and one that is already at considerable scale. The company's website claims 35m consumers have shopped using its payment methods, and says the service is live on 50,000 merchant sites and is processing 250,000 transactions a day. The business has raised over \$200m and, after Europe, is now focusing its efforts on the US.

The business, which is 10 years old, has further similarities to PayPal Credit and Affirm, in that it requires only a small amount of information to start the loan application. Further information is requested only if needed, radically simplifying the process from the applicant's point of view. A further benefit the service offers is the option to pay for the product after delivery, allowing time to review the quality of the purchase.

## 2.3 Savings and investments

After the day-to-day current account, savings are probably what most people think of when they think of retail banking. Two US startups help their customers take a proactive approach to encourage people to save. Digit connects with a customer's bank account and then, based on spending behaviour, automatically removes a small sum of money and deposits it in a savings account. It hopes to help put aside money that people wouldn't have otherwise saved, typically \$5-\$50 every two or three days. The business has raised \$13.8m to date and allows customers to withdraw from their savings account by sending an SMS. SMS is actually the main channel through which customers can interact with the service, with customers receiving a daily SMS of their savings balance, an option to receive a list of recent transactions, and the ability to pause, increase or decrease the saving plan. Due to its current regulatory status (as in, it's not regulated) it doesn't currently offer interest on savings, but it does seem to be gathering traction.

Similar to Digit, Acorns, another US startup, also automatically draws from a customer's account, although, in Acorns' case it deposits the money into an investment portfolio instead of a savings account. Acorns also takes a different approach to determining how much money to draw, by rounding up purchases to the nearest dollar and adding the difference to the savings. The company, which has raised $32m to date, reports 650,000 users.

The investment aspect of Acorns' proposition is similar to a series of online investment managers that have launched in recent years, a leading example of which is the UK's Nutmeg, which launched in 2012.

Nick Hungerford, the CEO of Nutmeg, says he wants to do to investing what Amazon did to retail – grow to dominate the marketplace and be available to everyone. Nutmeg welcomes customers with as little £1,000 compared with the £50,000 or more that a traditional fund manager requires.*

The business, which raised £19m in June 2014, reported having 35,000 active customers in Sept 2014. These customers are offered transparency with simple fees that range from 1% down to 0.3% and no set-up, trading, exit or other fees typically charged by the incumbents, as well as clear benchmarking and performance data.

Shaun Port, Chief Investment Officer at Nutmeg, says "we were starting with a clean sheet of paper. We had no legacy issues and could purely focus on clients and what is right for them". The company, which broke into the top 25 wealth managers in the UK, is starting to diversify as well with a pension product that launched recently.

Betterment is a US equivalent of Nutmeg. It was founded in 2008, and by the end of 2014 was closing in on $1bn in assets under management.

While it does cater to individuals looking to invest larger sums, much like Nutmeg, it also aims for a broad appeal by having no minimum investment requirement.

---

* http://citywire.co.uk/wealth-manager/news/wealth-manager-how-nutmeg-plans-to-become-the-amazon-of-finance/a677205

The service, which raised $32m in 2014, has fees starting at 0.15%, and on its website claims to offer 4.3% higher returns than the average DIY investor might expect. Their average user is in their mid-thirties but 20% of assets come from customers over 50. And, according to an article in INC Magazine, Betterment are able to acquire these customers at 25% the cost of their rivals.

They offer smart features, such as rebalancing, which automatically maintains portfolio balance while their tax-loss harvesting automatically offsets tax on gains with losses. While more recently the company launched Betterment Institutional, a service for advisers, presumably in an effort to get wider distribution.

Nutmeg and Betterment aren't the only companies operating in this space however. Rivals include Wealthfront, Personal Capital Advisors, SigFig and Wealth Horizon.

In a similar story to the the P2P start ups, our survey found that general awareness of these new saving and investment players appear to be low among the wider banking community.* 43% hadn't heard of Nutmeg and 35% knew the brand, but didn't know what they did. As with the digital challenger banks, executives in banks raised similar questions about the ability of these startups to scale to the level required to make their model work.

**Financial services products are sold, not bought. It will be interesting to see if these the online investment players can reach mass market at the scale they need to make their model truly economic and a serious threat.**

Anonymous banking executive

---

* Adaptive Lab / Research Now banking industry quantitative research study – Jan 2015

They're taking the technology of ETFs, a low-cost investing product, and packaging it with a low-cost portfolio construction service. But do consumers understand the value-add of their service? Do people trust the algorithm? Do people trust things online without a person, a face? It remains to be seen.

Anonymous banking executive

## 2.4 Payments

The payments market covers the interface between a customer and a merchant whether that be online or in a physical retail environment or as person-to-person payments, and is one of the most hotly contested areas for startups in financial services. In November 2014 AngelList, the investment website which tracks startups and the investment they receive, featured almost 1,500 startups in the digital payments arena alone. The payments market is broad so we'll just focus on two aspects – digital wallets and P2P models.

Digital wallets are devices or applications that allow people to make payments without using a card or cash. The digital wallet can be manually loaded with a balance, or else is connected to the consumer's bank account or payment card.

Since this is an intermediate step – a new middleman – between retailer and consumer, why does it appeal? There are a few reasons. PayPal, for example, is perhaps the best-known example of a digital wallet, and its growth was based on making online payments quick and simple. Yes, PayPal is an intermediary but it was easier to use than entering your credit card details for every purchase, and safer than allowing a retailer that you might not trust to store your credit card information. More recently, PayPal has launched a mobile app allowing consumers to make payments in physical stores too.

The strength of their brand when combined with the number of registered users and store cards makes them a formidable player. Even more so with their ability to make instant decisions to offer a line of credit following their acquisition of Bill Me Later, which we mentioned in the lending section.

Though digital wallets have been around for several years, use in physical retail environments has yet to take off. One of the barriers has been the limitation of technology at the point of sale in a shop or in a mobile phone. Until recently, Apple didn't have NFC (Near Field Communication) technology in its phones, for example, while merchants have to update their payment terminals to be able to accept payments. With this technology now available in the iPhone, the launch of Apple Pay is expected to boost consumer interest in the idea, while their recent partnership with Square will help with merchant adoption of the technology required to accept NFC payments.

> Mobile payments have been around for almost 10 years but haven't yet kicked off. The simple reason is that it's still easier for you to whip out your card to pay.
> **ALESSANDRO HATAMI**, former Lloyds executive

To ensure widespread adoption, though, the key will be simplicity. Apple has made paying with a mobile as simple as placing a finger on the iPhone's fingerprint sensor and tapping the phone against a payment terminal. While in the US this is a better experience than getting out a card, swiping and signing though, in the UK chip and pin is already quite quick and, for smaller payments, contactless is even faster so one might question, from a convenience perspective, will Apple Pay win out here.

Security, along with convenience, might be what drives growth in use as a recent survey by YouGov found that 55% of respondents felt that security of payment was the most important factor in choosing how to pay. With Apple Pay, security concerns are dealt with by ensuring that card details are not stored on the device or passed to the merchant.

Whether it's been due to convenience, perceived security or even novelty, as some surveys have shown, Apple Pay seems to have got off to a promising start in the US. One million cards were registered on Apple Pay in the first three days of its availability, which, according to CEO Tim Cook, made it the largest mobile payment system, with levels of activity reaching two of every three dollars spent via contactless payments on the three largest card networks in the US.*

Many observers also expect Apple Pay to kick-start a broader change in behaviour. If that happens, then rivals, such as Google, may see growing use of their own wallets. Supporting this thesis, Whole Foods Market, the grocer, has reportedly seen mobile payments of all kinds, and not just Apple Pay, increase by more than 400% since Apple Pay was introduced.

On the topic of changing behaviour, another recent Apple launch is likely to have a significant impact on their inroads into payments. Given that they have a knack of building out systems or ecosystems across several products, as demonstrated with iTunes, iPod and iPhone, Apple Watch is likely to even further improve on the experience of payment.

Whether paying with a watch or a phone, banks and payment scheme providers have expressed a concern about the 0.15% that Apple plans to take from each transaction. When this is taken into consideration alongside the planned change in the interchange fee, revenues generated by card swipes is going to be hit hard in the coming years, impacting this highly profitable aspect of the retail banking business model.

However, what might be even more concerning for the

---

* http://www.pymnts.com/in-depth/2015/tim-cook-2015-the-year-of-apple-pay

banks is not whether new entrants charge a percentage of revenue but whether they pursue an alternative business model altogether that sees them offering payments services for next to nothing, or even free. Google is perhaps seen as the most serious threat for this.

Google Wallet provides customers with a payment solution that lets you use your phone, but also gives some special offers at the point of sale.
Google are willing to give merchants a much discounted interchange rate because they were then able to link your purchase of a specific product to a previous search that you (the customer) had done. So that transaction would be funded through a cost-per-acquisition model versus the traditional cost-per-click model . . . but the merchant would get an interchange which is equivalent to a debit card interchange rate, which is pennies to pence to the transaction.

The step from there to nothing, from going from 3.4% to five pence to zero is very small. So you could see a future where all merchants will be told if the customer uses Google Wallet, it will be a free transaction.

Merchants will be very incentivised to get customers to use the Google Wallet. Therefore, they would create an environment where, first of all, it would be unsustainable for the bank to maintain interchange, but also they will lose the relationship with the customer because the customer will be using Wallet.

The objective of Google is not to create a payment solution. The objective of Google is to be able to address the issue that they're having, which is that the cost-per-click model is becoming less transparent of what benefit the advertiser is getting from that click.

In the case of Google Wallet, they can say, "Well, that customer that browsed X and Y, I can confirm to you that they went and purchased your product and here's the proof."

**ALESSANDRO HATAMI,** former Lloyds executive

A different type of payment is one made to friends and family and there's another group of entrants looking at this area, making it easier to repay a friend, for example after a restaurant bill. This is an inconvenience that most of us have experienced. You might not have the right amount of cash to pay your friend, so you agree to settle up later and then forget, or have to make a bank transfer, which in itself might force you into the poor user experience of a clunky security device.

US-based Venmo is one of the entrants gaining popularity in this space. Venmo has been described as a cross between Facebook and PayPal because of its newsfeed-style stream of transactions made between friends. While some audiences might be unsure about having transaction history data public, the transaction amount is actually hidden. Users say they like the service's easy way of calling in a loan by automatically sending a friend a payment request.

One customer told *Bloomberg Businessweek*: "I wouldn't scroll through Venmo just for kicks. But when I'm there, making a charge or a pay request, I like to check out what's going on. People are kind of entertaining. Everyone wants to be creative and sarcastic. It can be pretty funny." *

---

\* http://www.economist.com/news/special-report/21650297-if-you-have-money-and-even-if-you-dont-you-can-now-pay-your-purchases-myriad-ways

The app is so compelling that, according to Goldman Sachs, payment volume through Venmo is ramping up significantly from around $0.3bn in Q1 2014 to $1.3bn in Q1 2015. One of the reasons for this success is that payments in the US can take several days to process. In the UK, by contrast, P2P payments happen instantly, so success for a business like Venmo is more likely to be driven by the convenience, by not having to visit a bank website and avoiding using those annoying security devices.

Venmo was acquired in 2012 for $26m by Braintree, a company that enables online merchants to accept payments from cards, Bitcoin, Apple Pay and more. Braintree was later acquired by PayPal, which, like Venmo, also enables peer-to-peer payments in its app.

Square, founded by Twitter co-founder Jack Dorsey, recently launched a similar service called Square Cash, which, like Venmo and PayPal, enables a simple P2P payment. Unlike paying a friend through your bank, Square Cash doesn't require the recipient's bank details, just their mobile number, making the transaction far simpler.

Other than phone number, email address is another unique identifier, and a well-known tech giant recently launched a way to transfer a payment to anyone via email. Google has integrated its Wallet service into its email service, Gmail, making it simple to attach a payment to any email, even if the recipient is not a Gmail user.

P2P payment functionality is also being integrated into other messaging services. Square Cash powers Snapcash, a new payment feature in Snapchat the messaging app which, as of January 2015, reported 100m active users.

This should worry banks, as these payment companies can piggyback on large-scale existing behaviours and social networks. For the social network, it helps them become stickier but also presents an opportunity for them to branch out to become a wallet themselves.

And even bigger players are due to follow suit. Facebook, having applied for an e-money licence and, with payment-related code spotted in its Messenger app, seems poised to offer social payment features too. Might it also extend this to WhatsApp? Between these two messaging apps Facebook has a global base in excess of 1bn, which would make it a very serious player in the social payments and international remittance market.

From a bank's perspective this behaviour should be a worry because it's another action for which a customer doesn't need to visit a bank-owned channel.

## 2.5 International money transfer

Transferring money overseas used to be a time-consuming exercise and one that entailed lots of fees. Startups are changing that.

TransferWise is probably the most visible brand in international money transfer. It lets users send money to their own accounts or to other people worldwide but, instead of transferring the money, TransferWise matches it with transfers going in the other direction. To give an over-simplified example: if A, who is in the UK, sends £50 to B, who is in France, Transfer-Wise will find C, who is in France, and sending £50 to UK-based D. Then it will redirect C's money to B and A's money to D. In reality it doesn't work on matching individual transfers but larger, aggregated sums. The payment works smoothly for all users, but no currency conversion fees are necessary as the money does not cross an international border.

The business recently announced a new round of investment, which was led by Andreessen Horowitz, and valued the company at a figure in the region of $1bn. The service, which was founded by former Skype employees, reports an average transfer size of £1,300 and in its first year, 2011, facilitated

£10m in transfers. In 2012 this reached £50m and by March 2014 the service had transferred £240m in total. Since then the growth of the service has been hard to ascertain, but the company has raised close to $60m, suggesting that growth is heading in the right direction. In comparison, someone like Western Union facilitates around $70bn transactions a year, while the World Bank estimates total global activity of $529bn so it's clearly a big opportunity, of which TransferWise is only just scratching the service.

> TransferWise will succeed in those instances where they are less expensive than the bank transfer. The minute that they're not, which happens quite frequently – TransferWise is not always cheaper – the customer will not switch.
>
> **ALESSANDRO HATAMI**, former Lloyds executive

Azimo and WorldRemit are two similar startups from the UK, who have raised $11m\* and $147m\*\* respectively. WorldRemit says that 90% of its payments are received instantly rather than in a matter of days, which could be the case when using a traditional agent, not to mention the benefit of making the transfer via mobile rather than travelling to a branch. The service also offers the recipient a range of options for receiving the money – as cash in a bank account, phone credit or to mobile wallets. WorldRemit reports processing in excess of a million transactions a year, with an average transaction of around £200. Azimo, meanwhile, reports an average volume of £420. Azimo sends to 190 countries, while WorldRemit presently reaches 100.

---

\* https://www.crunchbase.com/organization/azimo

\*\* https://www.crunchbase.com/organization/worldremit

Despite some high profile advertising campaigns and securing funding indicative of belief in the growth of the international money transfer market, there still appears to be low level awareness of these companies amongst our survey respondents. 67% hadn't heard of Azimo and 26% knew the brand, but didn't know what they did. For TransferWise this was 51% and 35%.*

## 2.6 Money management

Another category of startups, Personal Finance Managers (PFMs) help people to better understand and track their finances.

> One of the areas that I think is very badly dealt with by the banks is the whole advice area. There has been, obviously, regulatory-wise, a crackdown on providing advice without disclosing to the customer that this advice is built up in the price of the item. There was a whole review of the retail practices of banks so they are retrenching from providing advice. That opens up completely the space of the provision of information on financial services to the customer.
>
> **ALESSANDRO HATAMI**, former Lloyds executive

Typically, these services allow users to aggregate their current, savings and credit card accounts to get a single view of their finances and categorise their spending and budget with built-in tools. They focus on functionality and utility, often offering a

---

* Adaptive Lab / Research Now banking industry quantitative research study – Jan 2015

better view of spending activity than retail banks' own websites and mobile apps.

Mint.com, a US-based startup, was one of the first, and was joined more recently by UK companies such as Money-Dashboard and OnTrees. Mint was founded in 2006 and acquired by Intuit, an accounting software firm, for $170m in 2009. By late 2013 it had claimed more than 10 million users in the US and Canada. OnTrees, meanwhile, launched in 2012 and was bought last year by price comparison service MoneySuperMarket for an undisclosed sum.

LevelMoney, which launched in 2012, is another US-based PFM which targets millennials looking to pay back student loans and to start saving. The business received $5m investment from VC KPCB and as of January 2015 had 700,000 users before it was acquired by Capital One.

A lot of investor attention is focused on the idea that PFM will make a huge difference to people's lives. I haven't seen any evidence so far to support this. Certainly there have been some nice kind of graphical interfaces and so on, but where's the proof that people radically shift their behaviour on the back of these tools and information? Getting customers to interact with PFM tools in the first place is hard. Getting them to do it regularly is even harder. This is because customers do not currently see value delivered to them by these tools.

**TOM HOPKINS**, Product Innovation Director, Experian Consumer Services

So far, none of the PFMs have achieved significant growth although it will be interesting to see if a simple, mobile-first offering, more closely integrated with a bank account can gain traction.

## 2.7 Money itself

It's not just aspects of the banking business model that are being challenged by new technology and startups. The idea of money itself is also being questioned by cryptocurrencies like Bitcoin. Despite the potential of the technology, many in the industry don't, based on the results of our survey, see it as something banks need to be considering with just 7% of respondents thinking that it should be.*

Bitcoin is a payment network and a decentralised digital currency that was invented by an unknown person using the pseudonym Satoshi Nakamoto. In a paper introducing the technology, Nakamoto describes it as an electronic payment system based on cryptographic proof instead of trust, allowing any two parties to transact directly with each other without the need for a trusted third party – a role typically played by a bank.

It was invented in 2008 but was open-sourced in 2009 and has since grown massively in use and profile. While traditional currencies are underpinned by central banks, trust in Bitcoins, which are mathematically generated, is ensured by a central log of every single transaction, access to which is open to the entire network. This shared public ledger is known as the "block-chain" and it works in such a way that each transaction builds on the one before. If the next transaction is fake, for example, then it will not fit the blockchain and will be immediately exposed. A transaction must be "signed" by the buyer using the secure private "key" – actually a code generated by algorithm – corresponding to their account, which is then verified by the network's public key.

---

* Adaptive Lab / Research Now banking industry quantitative research study – Jan 2015

In these currencies, coins are not issued by a central authority but "mined" by computers performing complex maths. Each time the computer completes work on a cryptographic key it is rewarded in new Bitcoins. As more coins are mined it becomes harder to mine new ones, requiring networks of computers and considerable amounts of time and electricity. Attempting to mine Bitcoins on your home computer, which was possible in the early days of Bitcoin, would now cost you more in electricity than the coins would be worth.

Bitcoin, which is known as a cryptocurrency because it uses cryptographic algorithms to ensure security, isn't the only digital currency. Darkcoin (designed to maximise privacy), Litecoin (designed to be faster) and Peercoin (aimed at being more energy efficient) are other examples.

These currencies are very new and not without problems. Most consumers do not understand them, for a start, which means that trust is low. There is a chance, however, that will soon change if they become regulated, as George Osborne suggested in his budget speech given in March 2015.

> I think it's an interesting idea. I think Bitcoin misunderstands the concept of currency and central bank, policy around currency, the way the currencies are actually used and inflation and all the other factors around it. I think it's a bit of a fad, a bit of a gimmick and a flash in the pan.
>
> Anonymous banking executive

Despite some in the industry thinking it's a fad, we're confident that Bitcoin and the cryptocurrencies that follow from it will have a significant effect on transforming not just finance but lots of other areas where transactions – share purchases, bets with bookmakers, property deeds and more – rely on verification by a trusted third party. The concept and design of the blockchain

# Unbundling the banking business model

Startups are attacking every aspect of the retail banking business model.

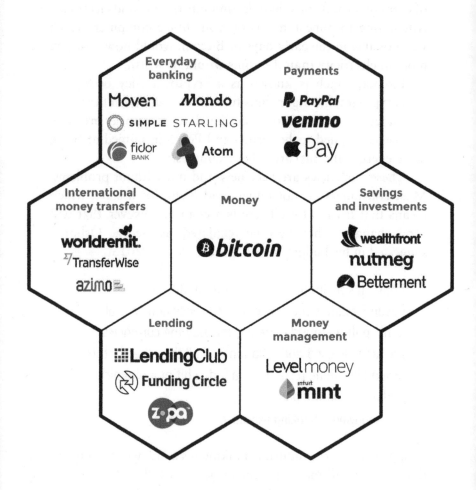

ensure that the transaction can be conducted securely for all parties, without the need for an intermediary. That represents a significant challenge to the financial services industry.

As this chapter makes clear, the retail banking business model is being well and truly unbundled, with new entrants taking aim at the high margins the traditional banks continue to enjoy. Looked at individually these new entrants should cause worry but, taking a step back, there is a broader scenario at play that we believe could pose an even more significant threat to the incumbents.

# 3. DISPLACED, DIMINISHED, DISINTERMEDIATED:
## A three-stage scenario that is underway

Among the numerous startups set to compete with the banks, there might be one that turns out to dominate, but from this vantage point it is impossible to know which. Our view is not dependent on there being one winner among the pack. The future might belong to a new company that grows to giant status and perhaps that company exists today or perhaps it is yet to be founded. However, even without such a company, we see a broader series of events at play, which, together with the sheer number of new competitors, should be of significant concern for the incumbents.

The events will take place as follows: Displace, Diminish and Disintermediate.

In this chapter we will describe those three stages, first using the example of the telecoms sector and the mobile network operators and then we will examine how they might apply to banking.

## 3.1 Displace

The first step in our scenario sees customer engagement and interaction shift from the incumbents to the new entrants because of the superior customer experience they offer and often a better price. In telcos this happened to the mobile networks with the arrival of the smartphone. At first, the networks and manufacturers controlled the customer interface on the phone. Later, as Internet adoption grew, they maintained control by deciding which Internet-powered services – news, sport, entertainment and so on – were accessible from their web portals and which companies would supply them. Likewise, the networks and manufacturers used to produce many of the applications installed on the phone and had complete control over which others shipped on the device.

The first challenge came when network operators allowed customers to access the web directly through a browser. This weakened their control but the next advance would blow it apart. In 2007, Apple launched the iPhone, and followed it a year later with the App Store. Suddenly, any developer could build an application and reach millions of people, giving consumers more choice than ever.

Some of these apps competed directly with core services provided by the networks. Messaging apps, for example, such as WhatsApp and Line, disrupted the networks' SMS and MMS business. WhatsApp offers features that go beyond the network service, including group messaging, quick and easy photo and video messaging, and status updates, and all for a cost of $1 per year, significantly cheaper than SMS rates.

Their impact can be seen in declining SMS and MMS volumes. Text messaging peaked in the UK in 2011 with an average of 228 monthly messages per person. By 2013, that had fallen to 170 per month – the lowest since 2008 – with messaging apps being identified as key drivers in the reduction.

This shift in activity has had a noticeable impact on the revenues of the networks. According to Ovum figures, phone providers worldwide lost $32.5 billion in texting fees in 2013. That trend also seems to have been reflected in the UK.* In August 2014, Ofcom attributed a £300m decline in 2013 UK retail mobile revenues – around 10% of the annual total – to declining SMS use. And it's not just messaging these services offer, as many of them have also launched video or video calling as well.

The result of this displacement is that the network becomes a "dumb pipe", providing the infrastructure for a service, in this case calls and data, but losing control of the customer relationship.

## 3.2 Diminish

The next step in our scenario sees the business model of the incumbents becoming even more challenged with their revenues diminished in an environment with increased frequency of switching.

The dumb pipe concept relegates networks to becoming a utility, with customers now lacking loyalty to any one provider and more inclined to switch between services. Services launched by two technology giants in the last year suggest how this might play out in the telco sector.

In the summer of 2014, Apple announced new iPads that came with a pre-installed SIM card, which they called a "Soft SIM". The Soft SIM makes it easy to switch between network operators to find the best reception at any time, without having to buy and switch SIMs. That removes a significant barrier –

---

* http://www.bloomberg.com/news/articles/2014-02-21/whatsapp-shows-how-phone-carriers-lost-out-on-33-billion

inconvenience and habit – that may have led people to avoid switching networks.

More importantly, this feature may be included in the next iPhone, and where Apple leads other vendors often follow. A SIM that automatically switches networks is ideal for customers who travel abroad, are seeking the best reception, and seeking the best rates. It's less appealing to the networks.

A new service from Google goes one step further, by handling network switching automatically. Project Fi, which launched in early 2015, allows customers to bridge two 4G networks and over a million free WiFi networks and does so seamlessly by scanning in the background for the next network to pick up so that calls aren't dropped and the customer doesn't even have to think about it.

These two launches demonstrate the power of owning the customer experience and how the incumbents could quickly be relegated to a utility (in a market with more frequent switching) perhaps just chosen on quality and price of service with no opportunity to differentiate otherwise.

## 3.3 Disintermediate

The final step in our scenario sees the core competency of the incumbent being challenged by the arrival of a new technology.

The idea of telcos being relegated to a utility is not a new idea. The term "dumb pipe" is often used, and the telcos talk about responding by being a smart pipe – attempting to differentiate by offering intelligent connectivity and value beyond just the data. But what if the core competency and strength of the telco, the pipes – or in this case the masts – is also challenged?

Over the last ten years, mobile networks have lost total

control of the customer experience but they retain the infra-structure – the radio masts that hold the transmission equipment and provide the network coverage that connects customer devices to the Internet.

What concerns the networks though is the ability to access data on the move in ways other than via the mobile network. One such change is already underway – the increasing provision of public WiFi. Many cities are rolling out WiFi coverage in central areas and that will only increase as installation costs fall. More businesses have decided that it makes commercial sense to offer WiFi to customers, drawing them to shopping areas, conference centres, cafes and restaurants. As already demonstrated by the launch of Google Fi, the availability of WiFi negates the need to connect to a network operator's mast, allowing the customer to save on data costs.

The second change, while not at the same scale, is likely to be more relevant in the future: the delivery of Internet connections via other means, such as satellites, high-altitude balloons or autonomous drones. For example, Google's Project Loon is using high-altitude balloons to deliver WiFi to areas with limited or no coverage. Balloons in the stratosphere create the network and pass the signal down to antennae attached to buildings. The company has begun experiments in New Zealand, and plans to provide coverage in Chile, Argentina and Australia.

Google and Facebook are also experimenting with drones that deliver WiFi, while various companies, including Virgin Galactic, Outernet and SpaceX are planning to launch low-Earth orbit satellites that would provide Internet access – in some cases free. Another kind of heavenly WiFi is being delivered in East Anglia by WiSpire, who are using church towers to deliver Internet connections across the region, that are poorly served by super-fast broadband. Beginning at Norwich Cathedral, WiSpire's signal is transmitted by hopping from one church tower to another, taking advantage of the height of the churches in the relatively flat county.

While the idea of WiFi delivered by balloons and drones might feel futuristic, ubiquitous WiFi doesn't seem unrealistic particularly when in a major city. This final part of the chain of events – the incumbent's core capability being challenged does not happen overnight and, in the case of telecoms, it is still far from complete. However, it allows us to describe a scenario that we can apply to banking.

## 3.4 The Banking Scenario

### 3.4.1 Displaced banks

> In theory, you could have your salary paid directly into your PayPal account by your employer and you wouldn't really need a bank account.
>
> Anonymous banking executive

As with telcos, banking incumbents are finding themselves competing with new entrants on customer experience and price. Many of the businesses covered in the previous chapter can offer a better experience and often a better deal because they're smaller, more nimble, prioritise design and are free of the legacy technology that an incumbent in any sector has to work with.

Might third-party applications lure customers away by offering core banking activities in a better user interface? It's not hard to imagine that a technology company can deliver a better payments experience than a bank. A survey in 2013 by payments firm Vocalink reported that 64% of UK consumers had made a mobile payment using PayPal, compared to 40% using their own banks app. Likewise, Apple Pay and other

# How retail banks are being displaced, diminished and distintermediated

The three stage scenario that we already believe is well underway.

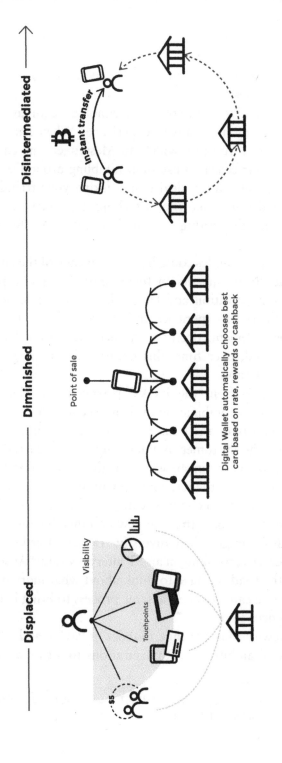

**Displaced**

Visibility

Touchpoints

$5

Day to day interactions move from bank owned interfaces to startups who offer a better experience or price.

**Diminished**

Point of sale

Digital Wallet automatically chooses best card based on rate, rewards or cashback

Business model under pressure as banks are relegated to utilities as switching frequency increases.

**Disintermediated**

Ƀ instant transfer

The core competency of the bank is challenged by the arrival of a new technology digital wallets offer a preferable experience for online or in-app purchases.*

In a similar vein, could a technology company deliver a better P2P money transfer experience? When Facebook rolls out that feature more widely in Messenger, one can imagine it will be far easier to use than fumbling around with a two-factor authentication device and asking your friend for their account details. Likewise, attaching a payment to an email you're already writing in Gmail would also offer this same ease.

Similar examples could be given for each of the banks' main activities. New entrants, by focusing on a smaller aspect of the banking proposition and free of legacy, are able to deliver a better customer experience and, often, price. In doing so they drive engagement, decrease the need to visit a bank-owned channel and, over time, this occasional activity could easily turn into a habit.

The risk from the banks' perspective is that the new entrants, or a combination of them, become the new customer interface, leaving the bank carrying the cost of acquiring and servicing the customer as interactions between the customer and the bank diminish, which further constrains the bank's ability to control the relationship with its customers and offers less opportunity to communicate, cross-sell and upsell.

A further risk is that the new entrants, having established a foothold might then diversify. Taavet Hinrikus, CEO of TransferWise, speaking in an FT interview said: "At some point down the road we have to think about what more we can do. Where else can we take the same process to bring better financial services to people?"

Likewise Max Levchin, founder of PayPal and Affirm, also has broad ambitions, with aspirations to create a full service

---

* http://www.euromoney.com/Article/3220677/VocaLink-database-could-give-mobile-payments-a-new-lease-of-life.html

financial institution. Levchin says: "We're trying to build the company that will service customers for their lifetime."

We haven't seen a huge shift in customer usage to the new entrants in financial services, yet. Due to a change in European regulation though, we believe that one of barriers, difficulty of access to customer account and transaction data, preventing this shift is set to be lowered.

The European Commission's Directive on Payment Services is intended to establish a single payments market across Europe, regulate previously unregulated companies and increase competition. An update, PSD2, will come into effect in early 2016 and will require banks to offer third-party companies access to their systems via Open APIs when a customer has securely authenticated with the third party.

> If the commission is successful in forcing the banks to open up the APIs, then for an awful lot of people it's just going to be a whole lot easier to go through Facebook, Apple, and Google to get to financial services than going to a conventional bank.
>
> **DAVID BIRCH,** Director, Consult Hyperion

Knowing the impact that APIs could have on the financial services market, HM Treasury published a paper on the topic in December 2014. The paper, which outlines the opportunities, challenges and best practices for banking APIs and Open Data, says: "It may challenge the behaviour whereby bank account customers often, by default, buy and use other financial services such as loans, mortgages, savings, foreign exchange and even online access from their core account providers."* In other words, challenge the fundamental business model of retail

---

* https://www.gov.uk/government/publications/data-sharing-and-open-data-for-banks

banks – running their current accounts as a hook to cross-sell lending products where they actually make money.

While the banks have some time before they have to comply with PSD2, some companies are already making it easy for startups to get access to a customer's bank accounts, and the activity around these services gives a hint of what might be to come. Yodlee, for example, enables OnTrees, the PFM MoneySuperMarket acquired to aggregate customer transaction data from multiple accounts. Plaid, another example, enables Digit, the automated savings app, to get authenticated access to the bank accounts of their customers. Plaid and Yodlee offer a well designed API for the startups to use albeit it one that currently violates the terms and conditions of the banks.

We believe the result of PSD2 will be to displace banks, pushing them away from the consumers and relegating them to providing merely the "pipes" of banking.

This is a very realistic threat. The likes of Google, Apple and others could potentially start pivoting their model to create a situation where the bank no longer becomes the owner of the relationship. For example, imagine if tomorrow Google decided to launch a banking aggregation system. You give your password and log in to your bank account, and they display the information to you in a way that is novel, more interactive, more user-friendly. You may decide that's a better way for you to manage your money than to log into your online banking. At that point, the relationship between you and the bank has changed.

**ALESSANDRO HATAMI,** former Lloyds executive

## 3.4.2 Diminished banks

As the new entrants succeed in replacing the banks' customer interface, we also see the banks' margins squeezed as they're relegated to the status of utilities. A status that leaves them with a reduced opportunity to communicate with their customers and little opportunity to differentiate in a market where switching increases in frequency.

> For the banks, the risk is that once someone takes away all of the interface, it may feel like less of a decision to switch. Perhaps consumers could eventually do it all in the background without dealing with the inconvenience of changing access codes or cards?
> **TOM HOPKINS**, Product Innovation Director, Experian Consumer Services

To illustrate this, let's go back to the examples of Apple's Soft-SIM and Google's Project Fi, which switch customers between carriers with great ease or even automatically. One clear equivalent in banking is a Personal Finance Manager that helps switch between accounts.

To demonstrate this, think of MoneySuperMarket which, following its acquisition of OnTrees, could, with relative ease, combine its product comparison data with a customer's own banking behaviour to prompt and enable switching.

And another example is already here. MaxMyInterest, a US startup that calls itself the "intelligent cash management solution", demonstrates a similar idea by helping maximise savings returns. The service, which is still at a relatively early stage, helps easily move customer's money between accounts to get the best interest rate at any point in time.

A further example, but around the payments interface, is

a digital wallet that automatically switches payment methods based on the rewards or cashback offered for that particular purchase. Apple Pay already stores multiple cards, allowing the customer to choose the one they want to use and with the release of iOS 9 will be recommending a specific card or loyalty card when in the corresponding retailer. It's not much of a stretch that Apple, or a similar company, extends this idea with a feature that automatically switches cards to get the best deal as PayPal are already doing, offering a new line of credit.

It's still early for both the PFM and digital wallet market, but if the consumer experience shifts to these new services they could, like Apple's Soft SIM, play a more dominant role, diminishing the power of the bank and empowering the consumer to switch between services more readily or even automatically.

> This is a very big risk. As the offerings of the banks are not that differentiated the relationship with the customer has a very high value, much more, potentially, than any other industries. There's currently an inertia with getting the customer to move from one bank to another . . . So if one of these startups make it easy for me to go from working with bank A to working with bank B, because in reality, you've created a layer on top that allows you to replace the bank on the back end but retain the relationship with the customer on your own, you are in fact destroying my revenue model.
>
> **ALESSANDRO HATAMI**, former Lloyds executive

### 3.4.3 Disintermediated banks

The final stage in the scenario sees the incumbent's core competency challenged by the the arrival of a new technology or tech player meaning even their role as a utility is under threat with the new entrants able to use alternative pipes. When we looked at telcos we outlined how their core capability, network delivered by mobile masts, was threatened by ubiquitous Internet delivered WiFi. Could the same happen in banking?

Some technology companies have pipes of their own that they could use to construct networks to rival the banks. Facebook, as mentioned earlier in this chapter, could do exactly that with Facebook Messenger or WhatsApp, turning them into payment networks with themselves as the trusted middleman.

Alternatively, a new technology could have a profound impact on the fundamentals of the banking model. Increasingly, it looks like the blockchain could have that impact.

In a paper published by the Bank of England called "Innovations in payment technology and the emergence of digital currencies", the blockchain is referred to as a first attempt at an Internet of finance. Consider for a moment, the impact of the Internet and how the concept of sharing information between computers has expanded far beyond anything its creators could have imagined. Now imagine a similar technology for finance, with unlimited potential to unleash change.

The current banking system relies on trust that each bank will maintain an accurate ledger and that the "clearing" service, which allows transactions between banks, will also process payments accurately. For clearing, the big banks still use technology that is over forty years old, called the automated clearing house (ACH). This batches transactions together and sends them out to be cleared at set intervals. A blockchain-based system would enable instant clearing, and it would be drastically cheaper and more secure too.

While there is both confusion over what the platform is and critique of whether it is viable, there are also a number of high profile people who do believe in the positive potential impact of it.

Oliver Bussman, the CIO of UBS, believes the blockchain could be the biggest disrupting force changing payments. He argues that when somebody with a strong brand and security level establishes it as a reliable service, then the whole industry will follow. If he is correct, then this is an opportunity for traditional financial services. However, what is likely is that new entrants that are able to move faster and with greater agility will be able to build services utilising the technology and might be able to leverage the cost advantage to explore business models alternative to the traditional banking model.

And just as Bitcoin has inspired other cryptocurrencies, so blockchain has inspired other similar technologies and companies, including Ethereum and Ripple. Ripple, which has already been adopted by some financial services organisations, has a shared public database ledger that acts as a kind of distributed currency market. Ken Kurson, writing in Esquire, wrote that Ripple, which is currently the second-largest cryptocurrency after Bitcoin, could do to financial services brands what Napster did to record labels in the 1990s.

This new technology concept, and what it inspires, seems set to have the same effect as the Internet did on fixed-line and mobile phone services, by making possible the likes of Skype and other VoIP services. By dramatically reducing the cost of individual transactions for which banks have traditionally charged a fee, and radically simplifying how money is stored and transferred, further reducing costs, they could ultimately force banks to alter their business models or, more likely, enable new competitors who are more responsive to the opportunities presented by new technology to create whole new business models on top.

These new companies are taking advantage of the forces of change we highlighted in the first chapter, building lean, agile businesses, ready to attack banking by displacing, diminishing and disintermediating the incumbents.

This stage describes the final step in our scenario, which we believe is already well under way. From our position it's not a matter of if this happens but when.

# 4. PEOPLE, CULTURE AND TECHNOLOGY:
# The challenges facing the banking industry

When setting out to write this book, we wanted to ensure that we took into consideration the opinion of those within the banks and working in the financial services industry. Through face-to-face interviews, a survey and a series of roundtable dinners, we were able to explore trends, challenges and opportunities. Some of this insight and opinion, as you'll have seen, has been interspersed through the book but three topics in particular came up as a recurring theme, which we felt required a separate focus in a standalone chapter. These topics are people, culture and technology.

Given the power of the quotes from our interviews we wanted to focus this chapter on these and provide minimal narrative around them.

## 4.1 People and Culture

> If you're a group MD responsible for P&L it's
> understandable you are not going to innovate or disrupt
> in a way that damages your P&L.
>
> **LEE SANKEY**, former Barclays executive

This is probably the most significant factor when thinking about change in large organisations. Some of the changes banks are facing require an incremental (albeit still challenging) shift, for example, the shift from a branch based model to a mobile one. While others are more fundamental, for example moving to a P2P model, which requires a complete rethink – a rethink that might result in a business that delivers a lower margin than what the bank is used to.

> Banks are massive businesses and to replicate what they
> (startups) do has the propensity to destroy the banks'
> internal business model and it doesn't immediately
> replace it with something that is as income generative.
>
> Anonymous Banking Executive

> The banks' current model is very profitable. So doing
> business the way they're doing business now has worked
> for them for many, many years. Suddenly throwing that
> away and replacing it with something that they're not
> certain about is scary.
>
> **ALESSANDRO HATAMI**, former Lloyds executive

This is further complicated by the fact that the process takes time. Large organisations are therefore faced with a paradox: they are too big to shift their culture very quickly, but their business is at risk if they shift too slowly.

One of the significant challenges to replicating one of the new models is the consequence on the banks' internal financial model. Do you choose to cannibalise yourself or allow it to happen slowly over a period of time. The complexities of how you migrate from one way of providing a service to another way of providing a service whilst taking the responsibility that you have to shareholder, stakeholder, marketplace, regulation, is incredibly complex. There's no simple answer that says, "We'll just replicate what's going on outside of your organization internally and everything will be okay".

**TRAVERS CLARKE-WALKER**, CMO, Fiserv Int.

I think this [challenge] is probably one faced by all large organizations, and particularly those which are successful today: you run the risk of not being able to do new things because of your focus on doing old things and trying to do them as well as possible. It is the central thesis of Clay Christensen's The Innovator's Dilemma. And it is made even more acute by regulation. In all of the major banks, there are hundreds if not thousands of people whose job it is to make sure nothing goes wrong for customers. This is literally programming the organization to not change. To grasp new opportunities in that setting requires a huge force of will.

**TOM HOPKINS**, Product Innovation Director, Experian Consumer Services

Regardless of whether the banks' are actually exploring new business models or not there is a view that they need to also rethink how they work more broadly if they are to keep to pace with the change they're experiencing outside their business. A fact that was highlighted in our survey – 69% of respondents didn't believe retail banks were able to react quickly enough to the changing consumer needs around digital servicing.

To help keep pace, many talk about new working practices such as design thinking, lean and agile, topics which came up in our interviews and dinners, but trying to embed these practices is found to be a real struggle.

The idea that incumbents don't understand what's happening is a myth. They have lots of great talent and ideas. Their challenge is implementing those ideas, especially at pace. Most sit in a PDF on a hard drive somewhere. These organisations are not used to working with lean, agile and design driven methodologies. They go against their DNA.

**LEE SANKEY**, former Group Design Director, Barclays

Internally it's a challenge for traditional banks, because the way they've grown up around regulation, the way they've grown up around waterfall style of deployment, the way they've grown up around internal stakeholder management, the way they've grown up around the necessary approvals, the expectations and how long projects take. It can be a blocker when trying to do new things.

**TRAVERS CLARKE-WALKER**, CMO, Fiserv Int.

At the moment, banks are set up to be very risk-averse, partly because of all the issues with the regulators. So whereas digital, by definition, is about taking risks and seeing whether things work. In banking, the kind of iterative process that is common at startups is actually quite difficult. In a bank, if you came in and said something like, "I have a 20% probability of working," you get kicked out of the office. Whereas in the digital space if people think they have a 20% chance of working, they give it a go. Then if it doesn't work, they try and work out why it doesn't work and then try and improve it.

Anonymous banking executive

You would have thought we would have adopted cloud computing. Why are banks still running servers? Because they're just afraid that their data in the cloud is too vulnerable. Whether or not that's true that currently is the view – that if you let something out, it's just too risky, that you need to own the servers and you need control.

Anonymous banking executive

What can help make the change to new ways of working is bringing in those who have experience of doing it elsewhere. People with digital and design experience, people who have grown up familiar with the technology and devices that drive the modern banking experience. The question that came up though was how well is the banking industry doing to attract them?

The biggest challenge in this sector right now is talent.
**ALESSANDRO HATAMI**, former Lloyds executive

> If you're a smart kid coming out of university, you're
> not going to work for a high street bank. You'll go and
> work for Google or for Facebook, or Apple or something
> like that.
> **DAVID BIRCH**, Director, Consult Hyperion

> Data and technology is where most innovation is going
> on in this world at the present. The people who are really
> creating waves in data and technology are not sitting in
> banks. They're sitting elsewhere.
> **ANNE BODEN**, CEO, Starling Bank

However, banks are making progress on this front and are
working to build the environments required to attract the types
of people they need. Even with the right people though, how
everyone is organised and incentivised is yet a further challenge
to overcome.

> There's nobody in the bank that's incentivised
> to maximise my [the customers] well-being over
> profitability. What people are responsible for right
> now is to maximise the return from the sale of cards,
> or maximise the return from the sale of loans. Now,
> the banks, by definition, create products that are in
> competition with each other. So cards and loans, for
> example, are competing. Investments and savings are in
> competition, for example. What happens, because of the
> way they're structured, different parts of the organisation
> are not able to think along the lines of customer need,
> and they're focused very much along product lines.
> So that makes it hard for a bank to back propositions

that are not about a product but only about customer experience or customer well-being.

Anonymous banking executive

Having somebody whose job is digital, in a bank, says a lot about the organizations in that it is something bolted on, rather than something that is fundamental.

**ANNE BODEN**, CEO, Starling Bank

Digital is often treated like a channel, thus missing the holistic opportunity. It's like taking a newspaper and putting it on an iPad. You've missed the point.

**LEE SANKEY**, former Group Design Director, Barclays

Overcoming all of these challenges is hard. Even more so when the leadership is themselves from a branch-based, pre-digital world. Our survey of banking executives found that just 21% of respondents felt their bank has a leadership that is knowledgeable about digital and this was also echoed in our interviews.*

The vast majority of the leadership of banks don't understand exactly how digital works. So they are very worried about the digital bank. They have a subset of their employee base running large percentages of their business without the leadership knowing exactly what's going on inside.

**ALESSANDRO HATAMI**, former Lloyds executive

---

* Adaptive Lab / Research Now banking industry quantitative research study – Jan 2015

These leaders have a personal challenge as well – if you have worked your way up through banking over a number of years then there is often little incentive to try a drastic change with the end of your career in sight.

> If you're nearing retirement why would you put the last years of your career on the line by doing something risky?
> Anonymous banking executive

## 4.2 Technology

Lack of agility in infrastructure was highlighted in our survey as one of the biggest internal challenges the banks face. Technology, like people and culture, unsurprisingly came up in every one of our interviews as one of the blockers to doing new things.

> We should be focused on creating amazing customer experiences rather than being tied to what current legacy platform/processes can support.
> **IAN BROMWICH**, Managing Director – Digital, Barclaycard

These legacy platforms are mainframes designed for a different era, to run branches when batch processing payments overnight was ok. Today the expectation is that everything happens in realtime and often on a mobile phone. The platforms have evolved but struggle to keep pace over time while their complexity has grown.

In a bank like Lloyd's, or RBS you've got a myriad of
systems and processes which have been joined up over
multiple layers, customer segments and channels. Then
you've got lots and lots of products. If you multiply
all the segments by all the channels and by all the
products, that's a tremendous amount of complexity.
This is compounded by the problem that you've only
got a limited number of people who know about those
systems.

**ANNE BODEN**, CEO, Starling Bank

This complexity makes it hard when wanting to explore opportunities like building APIs.

The existing banks have a huge technology challenge in
implementing Open APIs, because the service area is so
big. It is fundamentally the right thing to do for financial
institutions to have Open APIs but the problem is that
existing systems make it very difficult to do that.

Anonymous banking executive

I think that the banks' systems are not aligned or
cannot cope with simplifying data to the point required
to offer APIs. That's the problem. If I take a step back, the
banks are playing catch-up still. They're investing and,
by the time their IT projects are done, they'll be behind
the curve.

Anonymous banking executive

Despite this inflexibility there is clearly a burning desire from
those within the banks to deliver change to drive innovation,

however there is another driver for change which always has to be prioritised above innovation and that is regulation.

> Depending which bank you talk to, they will tell you that anywhere between 50% and 90% of their IT budget is being driven by regulatory changes. It makes change very difficult.
>
> Anonymous banking executive

> Big banks are spending half-a-billion to a couple of billion a year on maintaining those systems for regulatory purposes. So, imagine yourself in a big bank, the first thing you have to do is make sure you keep up with all the regulatory change. You may have to change those systems a hundred different times with a single change. Then you have to try and think about how you're going to give the customer a great experience. But if those customers sit across those products, getting that experience to be consistent and clear is a huge job, it's not easy. The banks are full of very, very clever people doing a great job. But what they're dealing with is a huge amount of legacy which is very difficult to deal with.
>
> **ANNE BODEN**, CEO, Starling Bank

In this chapter we've heard, from senior executives within the industry, some of the challenges traditional retail banks face is keeping pace with the change occurring outside their organisations. In the next chapter we'll outline what we believe the solution to be.

# 5. INTRODUCING A BETA BANK:
## How the incumbents can respond

What matters is not merely a competitive advantage at
a point in time but evolutionary advantage over time.
**GARY HAMEL**

In the previous chapters we've covered some of the new entrants unbundling the traditional retail banking business model,
and have introduced a scenario set to transform the banking
landscape. This scenario sees the incumbents *displaced* at the
interface, *diminished* as they're relegated to undifferentiated
utilities, before being *disintermediated* by the arrival of a new
technology that challenges the core competency of a bank.

We believe that scenario is already well underway, but
even if you don't agree, it's hard not to accept a few simple
truths: the pace of technology and consumer change that we
outlined in the first chapter is only going to increase; customer
expectations will only get higher; and competition is only
going to get fiercer.

> Five years ago you could write a multi-year IS strategy and be confident 80% would be right. That's no longer the case now as the market dynamics and pace have changed dramatically.
>
> **IAN BROMWICH,** Managing Director – Digital, Barclaycard

Once those truths are accepted then you can begin to plan a response.

## Embark on digital transformations:

Large, multi-year programmes of work to reduce cost/income ratios, to improve the customer experience, and try to adopt new ways of working.

## Invest in innovation:

Many banks have large internal innovation teams supported by specialist partners. These units explore new opportunities arising from changing customer behaviour, new technologies and business models by researching, designing and prototyping new services and products.

## Partner with startups, potentially through technology accelerators:

Incubators or accelerators run structured programmes to help early stage technology companies establish and grow their companies. The benefit to the startups is access to a small amount of capital, experience of the bank and, sometimes, preferential access to services or data from the bank. From the banks' perspective, they get exposure to new thinking and approaches, and could also acquire the company if they choose to.

**Create a VC fund to invest in startups:**

To realise some of the high growth that startups generate, banks have launched their own investment funds to make equity investments in the startups.

The banks are all already doing all of these things, but we're of the opinion that these initiatives will struggle to make a lasting or deep impact on the three key topics we covered in the last chapter: people, culture and technology.

> The reality of transforming massive companies is that it's really, really, really hard.
>
> **LEE SANKEY**, former Group Design Director, Barclays

To really create the culture, technology, and attract the best people that are required to build a bank relevant for the world as we know it today, an alternative approach is required, one that we are calling "the Beta Bank".

## 5.1 Meet the Beta Bank

### 5.1.1 Rethink

The Beta Bank is a fresh start, rethinking, redesigning and rebuilding a bank from the ground up to ensure it's fit for the future.

### 5.1.2 Separate

The Beta Bank is distinct from the parent bank, with a different HQ and a separate leadership with the freedom to make independent decisions.

### 5.1.3 Experiment

The Beta Bank is an experiment, not only in new products and services but also, more importantly, in new ways of working.

### 5.1.4 Digitise

The Beta Bank is a digital business from the ground up, not just in the services it provides but in its working practices and the way it views the world.

### 5.1.5 Design

The Beta Bank is design-led in its decisions and approach to problem solving and how it prioritises investment in superior customer experiences.

### 5.1.6 Focus

The Beta Bank isn't everything to everyone. It offers a few, brilliant and differentiated products targeted at well-defined customer segments and behaviours.

### 5.1.7 Open

The Beta Bank is transparent and open. Its business model is clear, its pricing is simple and its margins are public for all to see. This helps to build consumer trust and confidence.

The Beta Bank might sound like a big undertaking but there are sound business reasons for following this strategy. The primary reason is capital efficiency. Digital transformations can cost millions, or even tens of millions, in the planning phase alone, with vast sums spent on updating technology platforms. In contrast, the Beta Bank would, given its far leaner operating model, be much more efficient in its use of capital.

The independence from the main bank is another sound business reason for this strategy. While it might seem sensible to keep the experimental venture as close as possible, that is likely to be counterproductive. The parent company is likely to impede the progress of the Beta Bank with corporate antibodies – the forces, direct and indirect, that help to maintain company culture – attacking the new venture as well as overly influencing its direction.

There are several examples from other sectors that banks can look to for inspiration. Semco, a Brazilian firm that pursues this model attribute around two-thirds of their new products to satellite companies. *

More recent examples from closer to home include Hive, the smart central heating service created by British Gas, GiffGaff, the "virtual" mobile network owned by Telefonica, and Quote Me Happy, the insurance company started by Aviva.

## 5.2 Ten Steps to creating the Beta Bank

Ten years ago, I don't think any of us would have got anywhere close to imagining where we've ended up today. This is worth factoring in when you make predictions about the future. Especially when history tell us the rate of change has only ever continued to get faster.

**TOM HOPKINS**, Product Innovation Director,
Experian Consumer Services

Underpinning the Beta Bank are two core beliefs: its competitive advantage will come from adaptability and speed; and design will differentiate it from the competition.

---

* https://hbr.org/product/ricardo-semler-and-semco-s-a/an/TB0199-PDF-ENG

# The Beta Bank operating model

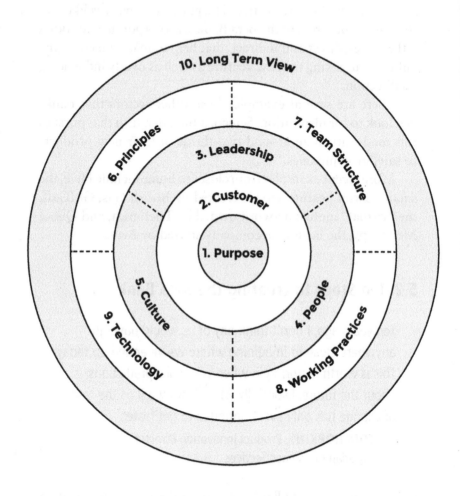

1. Define a purpose that inspires and attracts
2. Organise around customers rather than products
3. Appoint native leaders
4. Hire triple D people
5. Create a culture of experimentation and learning
6. Establish principles that inform decisions
7. Organise in small, multi-disciplinary teams
8. Design around modern working practices
9. Design technology and data that enables agility
10. Take a long term view

To act on those beliefs, here are the ten steps you need to consider for your Beta Bank.

### 5.2.1 Define a purpose that inspires and attracts

The Beta Bank is purpose driven.

Purpose describes the difference a company wants to make in the world. Companies with a clear, inspiring purpose attract not only great employees but also build a community of customers who believe in that purpose.

The impact of purpose was measured by Deloitte in a survey in 2013. They found that 90% of respondents who said their company had a strong sense of purpose also said their company had a history of strong financial performance. Those companies also enjoyed higher employee and customer satisfaction.

Tony Heish, of Zappos, introduced a purpose described as Delivering Happiness. He said: "A funny thing happened when we actually communicated this to our employees. We found that suddenly employees were a lot more passionate about the company, a lot more engaged and when customers called they could sense the personality at the other end of the phone wasn't there just for a pay check but really wanted to provide great service and when vendors came into our offices of visited us they wanted to stay longer and visit more frequently."

Successfully defining a company purpose across a large, established organisation is very difficult, but the Beta Bank has a clear, simple purpose from its inception, one that all its people understand and, importantly, believe in.

Examples of purpose are Google's "to organise the world's information and make it universally accessible and useful" and, closer to home, NewDay, the UK-based credit card issuer, which says its purpose is to "help people be better off financially".

A clear purpose also helps with focus. In the book *It's not what you sell, it's what you stand for*, Roy Spence, a co-founder of GSD&M, a Texas-based ad agency, and his co-author Haley Rushing, write: "You can look at an opportunity or a challenge, and ask yourself, 'Is this the right thing to do given our purpose? Does this further our cause?' If it does, you do it. If it doesn't, you don't. If it's proof to your purpose, embrace it. If it violates your purpose, kick it out on its ass."

Finally, a company's purpose plays a critical role in how it addresses change. If followed truthfully and relentlessly, it gives the opportunity to rethink a business model in pursuit of the purpose rather than stick to what it's done previously purely because of habit or a prior investment in technology.

### 5.2.2 Organise around customers rather than product

The Beta Bank is customer, rather than product, orientated. Instead of starting from financial services products, like current accounts or mortgages, the Beta Bank designs its services based on the needs and behaviours of its target customers, the lifestage they're at, and the journey they're on.

Being customer – rather than product – orientated not only enables a better service and experience to be designed, but can also help ensure that the Beta Bank isn't wedded to a legacy product or technology, which is important in times of great change.

Theodore Levitt, formerly editor of *Harvard Business Review*, introduced the idea of being customer-orientated in an article titled "Marketing Myopia". Levitt talks about how the railroads in North America went into decline because "they were railroad orientated instead of transportation orientated". Likewise, he wrote about how Hollywood faltered following the arrival of TV because it thought it was in the movie business rather than the entertainment business.

To give an example of the norm within a bank today, it's not uncommon for a customer to have five financial products with one bank and, while they of course know that, the banks struggle to. This surfaces itself in a number of ways. First, when contacting a call centre the agent may not be able to access all the information about a customer and their accounts. Second, when looking to access the information online or through a mobile app, all the information might not be available for the customer to see in a single view, requiring visits to different websites with separate logins. All this leads to a less than favourable customer experience.

> So if you go inside a bank, you and I are not seen as you or I. We're seen as buyer of mortgage on X street and owner of credit card Y, et cetera. So I can have four different products and be seen as four different customers. There's nobody in the bank that's incentivized to maximize my well-being or my profitability. What people are responsible for right now is to maximize the return of the sale of cards, or maximize the return from the sale of loans.
>
> **ALESSANDRO HATAMI**, former Lloyds executive

To avoid this and to be truly customer-orientated, the Beta Bank ensures it fully understands its customers and that this knowledge is dispersed throughout all levels of the business. A couple of examples from the tech world demonstrate how this is.

In a recent *Wired* article, AirBnB's Head of Design, Alex Schleifer, shared the opinion that companies should place at least one person whose sole role is to represent the user in every team.*

---

* http://www.wired.com/2015/01/airbnbs-new-head-design-believes-design-led-companies-dont-work/

Another example from AirBnB illustrates the importance of experiencing a product or service as a customer. Brian Chesky, one of the co-founders, took this idea to the extreme in the early days of the company, as he lived, for a period of time, entirely in properties and rooms he rented through his site, to experience what it was like. This mentality helps to build the required empathy to be customer orientated, as well as being a good signal from the leader to the rest of the organisation of its importance to the company.

In a similar vein, Steve Jobs used to talk about the importance of "staying beginners". By this he meant constantly trying to look at products as if they're being experienced for the first time. A result of this was Apple shipping its products with charged batteries so people could use them straight out of the box.

### 5.2.3 Appoint native leaders

The leadership of the Beta Bank would not only be literate with the way the world works today but also native to it.

Burberry is one example of a company that understands the importance of native leadership. Its Chief Executive, Christopher Bailey, had first joined the business as Design Director, before being promoted to Chief Creative Officer, and then CEO. When looking at the tech startups that are starting to compete with the banks though, native leadership isn't the exception, it's the norm.

Analysis by John Maeda, design partner at VC KPCB and former President of the Rhode Island School of Design, demonstrates the growing number of high growth, design-led companies, which shows that, in addition to deep technical experience, these businesses also champion design as a skill.*

---

* http://www.kpcb.com/blog/design-in-tech-report-2015

Since 2010, twenty-seven startups acquired by the likes of Google, Facebook and Yahoo! were co-founded by designers. Meanwhile, an increasing number of the top VC-backed companies have designer co-founders.

The leader of a Beta Bank is confident talking about topics ranging from ethnographic studies, APIs to AB testing. That's not to say they don't have a banking background, but being a digital native with a little banking experience is preferable to being a banking native with a little digital experience.

Capital One is an example of a well-known financial services company that already values design leadership, as demonstrated with the hire of Dan Makoski, who had previously been at Google's Advanced Technology and Projects Team. They're an outlier, though, in contrast to the leaders at many of today's fast growth companies.

Not only is the Beta Bank's leader experienced in digital and design but they are also a magnet for the best talent in the design and technology world. While there aren't many leaders like Elon Musk, who co-founded PayPal and has since gone on to found Tesla, SpaceX and SolarCity, he is a good example of the kind of individual who attracts further brilliant people to a company.

The fine line the leader of the Beta Bank treads is one of inspiring and driving forward, but balanced with understanding the importance of letting go and giving her team autonomy. Perhaps the most extreme example of this kind of distributed decision making comes from Semco, the Brazilian conglomerate, which actively celebrated the tenth anniversary of the date the CEO Richard Semler last made a decision.

Likewise, when asked about how he drove the success of his company, Southwest Airlines, Herb Kelleher, said: "Well, the people did it. I just stayed out of their way." Further evidence of this way of thinking comes from Ilkka Paananen, the CEO of Supercell, a highly successful Finnish gaming company who says his goal is to become "the world's least powerful

CEO" in an interview with *Wired* magazine, in reference to his view that teams should be empowered instead of dictated to.

### 5.2.4  Hire Triple D people

The success of the Beta Bank will be based on the quality of its people. The Beta Banks people will be Triple D: Design-focused; Digitally native, and Diverse in their background.

By design-focused, we mean that they ask why, they frame problems from the customer's perspective and context, rather than that of the business, and they they solve problems through making and prototyping. Digital natives are those who understand the digital world, have grown up with it and intrinsically get how it works. Finally, diversity brings different views to problems as empathetic thinking is more achievable when a broader set of people are represented within the organisation.

While the type of people is important, the quality of these people is critical. Patty McCord, who was chief talent officer at Netflix from 1998 to 2012, wrote in an article for HBR: "The best thing you can do for employees is hire only 'A' players to work alongside them. Excellent colleagues trump everything else."* To support this belief the company also has a rich severance package that allows it to discharge people who don't cut it as A players.

Attracting these A players isn't easy, though, so the Beta Bank is designed from top to bottom in a way that helps it attract the best.

Daniel H Pink, the author of *Drive*, a book on motivation, talks about the idea of motivation 3.0. Pink says that these days, employees seek autonomy, mastery and purpose.

Spotify offers an example of autonomy which although may seem small makes a big difference to the type of people

---

* https://hbr.org/2014/01/how-netflix-reinvented-hr

they, and the Beta Bank, want to have working with them – its software engineers can choose the tools that they use to develop software, rather than having them mandated by the company, which is often what happens in large corporates.

Mastery refers to the human desire to improve something that matters to us, and Spotify again acts as a useful example when talking about this. Its staff is organised into so-called squads, tribes, chapters and guilds. The guilds in particular are interesting, as they are interest groups that are formed across the company, allowing people to share knowledge, working practices and tools. This loose structure encourages and enables learning and self-improvement.

We've already touched on the notion of purpose but its importance bears repeating. Elizabeth Moss Kanter, a professor at Harvard Business School, who has researched a number of companies that demonstrate high capability with respect to innovation* says that "people can be inspired to meet stretch goals and tackle impossible challenges if they care about the outcomes".**

There is a final "D" quality that is worth mentioning here – the "Deviant". The Deviant in this context will question the team's assumptions, rebel against conformity and be willing to ask "wait a minute, why are we even doing this at all?" This was a role that Steve Jobs frequently played at Apple, for example, especially in the company's early years. Every team should have a deviant.

### 5.2.5 Create a culture of experimentation and learning

The Beta Bank's culture doesn't just permit but actively encourages and champions, experimentation.

---

* https://hbr.org/2011/11/how-great-companies-think-differently/ar/1
** https://hbr.org/2013/04/to-find-happiness-at-work-tap/

The idea of experimentation is one that that is deeply ingrained in the psyche of technology companies. In a 2014 shareholder letter, Jeff Bezos, founder and CEO of Amazon highlighted their commitment to experimentation, explaining that the volume of experiments performed under its Weblabs initiative, which it uses to evaluate website and product improvements, grew from 546 in 2011 to 1,092 in 2012 and 1,976 in 2013.

Likewise, Google also champion the idea of experimentation. Eric Schmidt, their executive chairman, says: "Our goal is to have more 'at bats' per unit of time and money than anyone else."

Having a good source of ideas for experiments is something that the Beta Bank prides itself on. The diversity of its people and their backgrounds helps, but the Beta Bank furthers this search by looking at the edges, at extreme customer groups, different geographies and alternative sectors. For example, what can be learnt by studying mobile behaviour in Asia? Or how the gambling industry acquires customers online?

The opportunity presented by experimentation is not just improvement but also valuable learning. Tom Chi who works at Google X, the division at Google responsible for their so-called "moonshot" projects such as Google Glass and the driverless car, says that he believes that no failure is a 100% failure. Instead, a failure might have 5 or 10% success. Teams learn from each small success so that, over time, teams learn a huge amount from these apparent failures. Instead of fail fast, Mr Chi prefers the phrase "learn fast" and talks about increasing the frequency of experiments to maximise the rate of learning.

To maximise learning the Beta Bank is designed to run experiments with ease and with technology that enables experimentation, the right metrics to measure outcomes, and customer communities to run pilots with lots of luck.

The Beta Bank runs experiments not only around its current (digital) product and proposition, by exploring new features and customer journeys both in test and in live environments by doing what's called multi-variate testing, but also around future propositions allowing it to test potential new business models.

## 5.2.6 Establish principles that inform decisions

If the company's purpose is what drives it in the long term, then its principles, along with the people who enact them on a daily basis, are what help establish the culture to fulfil on that purpose.

Clear principles help the Beta Bank to move at speed, because they distribute decision making, allowing teams to make decisions autonomously.

The Beta Bank's principles are clear and understandable – just like its purpose – and over time they become illustrated with stories and examples of how they have been used, which helps propagate the culture in the company.

The Government Digital Service, which is responsible for the digital transformation of the government, is an example of an organisation that has established a clear set of principles that inform how they work and make decisions. One of their principles is do the hard work to make it simple which prompts their teams to think about how to simplify the services that they're designing to ensure they can be easily used by the diverse customer groups that they serve.

It is easier to define principles than it is to adhere to them, and for that reason the Beta Bank knows that employees should play a key role in establishing the principles. An important part of recruitment, therefore, will be finding people who share the same ideology.

While principles inform ways of working and decision

making, a focus on outcomes ensures teams are aligned with success and what it looks like. Discussing outcomes not only helps with alignment but, if accompanied by a trusting and empowering working environment, also enables teams to make their own choices about how to reach those outcomes rather than a solution or approach being prescribed.

As the famous quote by French author, Antoine de Saint-Exupéry, goes: "If you want to build a ship, don't drum up people to collect wood, don't assign them tasks and work but, rather, teach them to long for the endless immensity of the sea".

## 5.2.7 Organise in small, multi-disciplinary teams

The Beta Bank is designed from top to bottom to ensure its agility. Its ability to develop new services quickly and to continuously improve those already in market is made possible by the way it designs its teams.

These teams are small – and deliberately so. A number of examples of highly successful organisations coupled with academic research show why smaller teams are more effective, and why teams at the Beta Bank would rarely be bigger than six to eight.

Supercell, the Finnish gaming company, has teams of five to seven it calls cells, hence its name. Yammer, a tech company acquired by Microsoft for $1.2bn, favours teams of between two and ten people. Spotify's teams are typically fewer than eight people.

And it's not just tech companies adopting this approach. The CIO of GE Capital, Jim Fowler, who himself has a workforce of 4,500 in a larger organisation of around 300,000, believes that teams of about ten are optimal.

There are four key reasons why small teams are better.

**Communication and co-ordination is harder.** As teams grow, more time is required to keep all team members informed, and more opportunities arise for misunderstandings.*

**Teams think bigger is faster.** Academics have identified a problem known as the team-scaling fallacy, which causes teams to underestimate how long a task or initiative will take because they think bigger teams are more efficient.**

**Feeling of stress can arise.** Relational Loss is a concept that explains the importance of cohesion and relationships in teams. Individuals feel that as teams grow they lose support, which would buffer stressful experiences as well as help encourage positive performance.***

**Social loafing** is the tendency for individuals to expend less effort when working collaboratively than when working individually.****

The Beta Bank's teams will not only be small but also multi-disciplinary. Marty Cagan, the founder of Silicon Valley Product Group, who held senior management roles at the likes of AOL, eBay, Netscape and HP Labs, describes an ideal team as featuring a product manager, user experience design, project management, engineering and product marketing roles.

Multi-disciplinary teams are able to move faster, because all the necessary skills and capabilities are present, meaning the team aren't dependent on other teams or groups in the company. Furthermore being dedicated rather than spread

---

* https://hbr.org/2009/05/why-teams-dont-work
** http://public.kenan-flagler.unc.edu/Faculty/staatsb/neglect.pdf
*** http://www.sciencedirect.com/science/article/pii/S0749597811001105
**** http://psycnet.apa.org/?&fa=main.doiLanding&doi=10.1037/0022-3514.65.4.681

across several projects, as can often be the case, also helps with speed.

## 5.2.8 Organise around modern working practices

At the Beta Bank the digital product development teams are the true engine of the business so the whole company is designed around them. We've already covered the size and composition of the teams, but for them to do great work, the way that they actually work is of equal importance.

The Beta Bank draws from several schools of thought when developing products, namely design thinking, lean, agile and continuous delivery. Let's explain those a little.

**Design thinking** sees problems explored from the perspective of the target audience, with solutions to their needs and behaviours arrived at through divergent thinking, rapid prototyping and testing with real users.

**Lean and, specifically, the lean startup methodology** outlines a build, measure, learn cycle and suggests that a minimum viable product (MVP) should be released as early as possible, enabling valuable customer feedback to be gathered quickly to validate thinking before costly investment. This learning is then taken into consideration for the next version of the product.

**Agile development** sees requirements planned, designed, delivered and tested regularly through short iterations, as opposed to planning and design being conducted first and then lengthy development and testing at the end. This allows for frequent feedback and a reassessment of priorities and requirements on a regular basis.

**Continuous delivery** is an approach used in software development to improve delivery through automation of tasks such as testing, and increasing deployment frequency.

The thread that runs through all these is the end customer and their importance to the process, ensuring they're part of the journey from problem through to product in market.

While new to banks, these ideas are starting to take hold, but the biggest challenge is that the approaches are being squeezed into or around other systems and processes (risk, finance, compliance). The Beta Bank champions the importance of the right way of working, so starts with this and then designs the other processes around the model way of working.

## 5.2.9 Design technology and data that enables agility

One of the biggest challenges that the incumbents in banking, or any sector for that matter, face is their legacy technology – large systems that have been built over time and have grown more complex with the addition of new products, markets and channels. Technology has evolved, though, as have technology design practices so, much like the Beta Bank designs its teams, it also designs its technology for adaptability and speed.

For a Beta Bank, while customers certainly come first, data and API design come a close second, given their importance for driving software that is flexible and interoperable. Well-designed APIs that come with well-designed documentation, consoles and test environments replace the need for custom integrations and time consuming face to face meetings and enable internal teams to move much faster.

Not only that, APIs also create opportunities to engage with partners and third parties to build applications on the bank's technology and data. A Beta Bank understands the importance of owning the customer interface but also that it can't own all of them, especially with new players always emerging, so by offering APIs it can power all the interfaces where its customers are and that banking services are relevant.

Facebook's platform is one of the most impressive examples of this, with an API strategy at scale that has created significant benefits. Billion dollar companies have been built on top of Facebook, utilising their API platform. These companies have delivered new experiences for Facebook, which helps Facebook retain their customers and often generate new revenues.

Salesforce.com is another example of a business that's realised tremendous benefits through its open API strategy. The cloud computing company that offers Software-as-a-Service to enterprises generates 50% of its revenue through its APIs. For another, eBay, the online auction site, that total is 60%.

Jeff Bezos supposedly decreed that all Amazon teams expose their data and functionality through APIs, with a view that one day they might be exposed externally. Werner Vogel, Amazon's CTO, goes on to say this requires that "each of these services require a strong focus on who their customers are, regardless of whether they are external or internal".

While the initial benefits of APIs are realised by the Beta Bank, ultimately their customers realise them through having their needs better served both by the bank, which is able to deliver product innovations faster, and third parties, who are able to offer banking functionality through other interfaces or services.

## 5.2.10  Take a long-term view

If we were to suddenly decide that we're going to be a digital bank, what would that mean to how we sell in branches? Should we be shutting some of them down and change the user experience in them and so on and so forth. Intellectually, that's a discussion the banks want to have. In practice, it involves heavy lifting. It requires not only conceptually identifying a completely different business model, but also laying people off, restructuring infrastructure, investing in real estate, et cetera, et cetera, et cetera. Which is stuff that's very tricky in an environment that you're focused about generating the revenues for the next quarter. You're not thinking about what's going to happen in three years' time.

**ALESSANDRO HATAMI,** former Lloyds executive

The Beta Bank takes a long-term view, which is critical for a number of reasons. The first is that it helps align shareholder and customer interests.

In 1997, Jeff Bezos, told investors that Amazon was focused on the long term. He said: "If you're long-term orientated, customer and shareholder interests are aligned. In the short term, that's not always correct." In other words, when companies make decisions based on the next quarter's results, they are prioritising share price and not value to the customer which may lead to the right outcome for one important stakeholder but potentially a negative one for an ultimately more important group.

To make this work, two key things need to be reconsidered. The first is employee incentives, while the second is investor relationships.

Zappos, the American shoe retailer, is another example of a company that takes a long-term view and incentivises its staff accordingly. Tony Heish, Zappos CEO, says that if a customer calls looking for a product they don't have in stock, they will find the product on a competitor website and direct the customer there. He says: "In the short term we're going to lose that transaction . . . but we're not trying to maximise for every transaction. We're trying to maximise the customer experience and build that lifelong relationship with customers." In a similar way, when designing the structure of a Beta Bank, the incentives of employees at all levels need to be aligned with longer term outcomes that balance customer value and positive impact, along with profit.

This balance is one that investors also need to be understanding and supportive of. Bezos communicated his long-termism to investors from the beginning, which enables him to continue to pursue this strategy. A Beta Bank also secures this support from its investors.

Taking a long-term view also means investing in people and culture. The types of people that are needed to build a company that can compete in today's technology and design-led world are in high demand, so take environment into consideration when picking their next challenge. A concerted focus on culture allows the Beta Bank to create the type of workplace where great people want to work and where they can develop their skills and do their best.

Finally, and most importantly, the long-term perspective means the Beta Bank is not only attuned with the increasing pace of change but is designed to be responsive to those changes as they happen and positioned to bridge business models as required. All of the points comprising the operating model for the Beta Bank that we've outlined have been included with that in mind.

# 6. SUMMARY

Changes in technology, consumer behaviour and the competitive landscape have impacted every aspect of our lives and radically changed the environment for the companies that have traditionally provided services to us. A wave of software businesses is transforming sectors, from taxis to hotels to telecoms. As this book explains, a similar wave is now hitting banking too.

We opened with a quote from Bill Gates and, to those who doubt our thesis, it's worth keeping in mind another of the Microsoft founder's maxims: "We always overestimate the change that will occur in the next two years and underestimate the change that will occur in the next 10."

While we haven't yet seen the WhatsApp or Uber of banking, what is likely is that one is probably already under our noses. And what is even more likely is that, for now at least, it won't look like a bank. It will do one small aspect of the banking model and do it far better than anyone else.

We've covered a number that are doing just that. Targeting specific areas of banking, and doing so with a different mindset and a customer-focused approach. Businesses like Funding-Circle and TransferWise are taking the banking model apart and are able to excel because of their narrow focus, rethinking the experience, distribution and operating model. And their growth is accelerating, all while more new entrants arrive with even greater funding available.

Over the next ten years as an increasing number of these new startups arrive we believe a series of events will play out in a way that will have a massive impact on the incumbent banks. This is how the scenario plays out: first, the banks are displaced by new entrants offering better customer experiences and price. Then their revenues are diminished, as they're relegated to a position of an undifferentiated utility in an environment with higher rates of switching. Finally, the arrival of a new technology, like the blockchain, challenges the banks' core competency, as the new players bypass their services, disintermediating them entirely.

Even if you believe that the startups we've listed in this book could never topple a bank, even if you don't agree with our scenario that banks will be displaced, diminished, disintermediated there are a couple of things you surely can't doubt.

First, that more new technology is on the way which will have a significant impact. Though mobile devices and digital technology have changed the way we bank, they have not really changed the behaviour underlying banking itself. However, machine learning and artificial intelligence, which will be available at scale at marginal costs, will provide banking services that are personalised and constantly adapting. What's more the true impact of the blockchain is still not fully known. The real paradigm shift might be still to come.

Second, there is a whole generation of new banking customers who from birth will have been exposed to smart devices, the Internet and more. How can we possibly imagine what their banking behaviour will be like and who they'll trust to deliver banking services?

Compounding this is the regulatory environment in the UK and EU, adding power to the perfect storm hitting the retail banking business model. What once protected the banking industry and formed a barrier to entry is being reduced by governments seeking to drive competition and innovation through measures such as a simplified banking authorisation, PSD2 and changes to the interchange fee.

The banks, despite being confident of their position, see the change happening around them and are investing heavily in reinventing themselves, but they will struggle to truly do this because of challenges related to people, culture and technology.

Technology originally put in place many decades ago to manage branches now has to serve new channels that didn't even exist when it was created. Years of change and complexities due to diverse products, markets and channels leave these platforms creaking while they face a further backlog driven by compliance rather than innovation.

Culture, too, is something that evolves over many years – hundreds, in the case of banking. The cultures at successful companies enable them to excel at executing the business model they've always known. But they become risk averse as they protect this business model and accordingly it is almost impossible for banks to "think like" startups, because they are hard-wired to repeat the things that they've always done.

And that brings us to the people. Even if banks are able to hire the right ones, it's a huge barrier to overcome the risk averse culture, bureaucracy and traditional approach to delivering change. How do you convince a senior manager to authorise a project that threatens her department or, god forbid, her bonus? And how do you instil a change that gets an organisation of thousands to think like a lean startup of a dozen or so?

We believe the obstacles banks face are too great for them to overcome from within. Instead, they must reboot and create an autonomous organisation outside the bank itself, something we call the Beta Bank. It will be a business that, from the ground up, is designed to be able to handle a continually changing world. It knows that speed is its competitive advantage, while design and experience are what differentiates it.

Despite being designed for speed and adaptability the Beta Bank has a long-term view towards creating a sustainable model with customer value rooted in its purpose. In pursuit of this it looks beyond short-term profits, focusing instead on taking decisions that advance that long-term goal.

The Beta Bank is an organisation led and staffed by design-focused, digital natives. The whole business is organised around a new product-development approach, which has customers at its heart. A culture of experimentation and learning allows its small, multi-disciplined teams to explore new ways of working, experiences and business models. Its operating system is driven by APIs, embedding it in a network of companies and technologies.

The Beta Bank learns from the new generation of software businesses. It is transparent in its policies, fees and purpose, so as to establish the trust of customers who are sceptical of the banking industry. And is constantly improving its services and rolling out improvements for a generation raised on the annual upgrade.

Mark Zuckerberg, Facebook founder and Chief Executive once said: "The biggest risk is not taking any risk . . . In a world that's changing really quickly, the only strategy that is guaranteed to fail is not taking risks."

There are of course some important questions that the model we've outlined doesn't answer and that would need to be considered. For example, whether the Beta Bank should be later subsumed by the parent or instead whether customers and teams should be migrated across to the business or if indeed either should happen. Another although certainly not the last unanswered question would be if and how the parent brand is used.

Despite these unanswered questions we strongly believe that pursuing the model we've outlined to launch a Beta Bank is a risk that banking leaders need to take. We believe the model is the only way to build a business with the people, culture and technology needed to survive in a world increasingly led by the likes of Mark Zuckerberg.

So really the question is: are you ready to design your Beta Bank?

# REFERENCES AND FURTHER READING

We've included footnotes throughout the book but to make it easy for you to look them up we've also put them online at the following URL along with some other great reads on the topic.

**http://bit.ly/readlistsbyebyebanks**

If you're interested in further reading around the topic you may also be interested in a Flipboard magazine we curate called *Bye Bye Banks*. You will find articles being added regularly covering news from interesting startups as well as what the incumbents are doing.

**http://bit.ly/byebyebanksflipboard**

This book is brought to you by Wunderkammer, the publishing arm of Adaptive Lab.

 **ADAPTIVE LAB**

Adaptive Lab are pioneering digital product and service specialists.

Accelerating change in technology and customer behaviour is transforming every sector of the economy. With new competitors emerging virtually overnight, success is dependent on a company's ability to embrace disruption.

We partner with forward-looking leaders who recognise the imperative to rethink as the world around their company changes. We help to transform their existing businesses and to develop new propositions by deploying the smart-working methods of the world's fastest growth tech startups.

Our clients include Associated Press, Barclays, Barclaycard, Experian, Johnston Press, Tesco, Three Mobile, and Vodafone.

*"I have worked with many of the leading design and consulting companies and Adaptive Lab is right up there. Their combination of user centric product development and lean thinking not only delivered valuable technical, design and strategic insights, it demonstrated the new way of thinking and working that is essential for any company that wants to keep pace in today's fast- moving landscape."*

**- Boe Hartman, CIO - Barclays Bank, Barclaycard Operations & Technology**

Get in touch to discuss how Adaptive Lab can help your business.

hey@adaptivelab.com

www.adaptivelab.com

020 3772 4630

Adaptive Lab
91 - 93 Great Eastern Street
London
EC2A 3HZ

You may also be interested in...

### Join one of our Curious Dinner roundtable discussions

Adaptive Lab regularly hosts a number of roundtable dinners where we assemble a group of senior executives from a range of top corporations and ambitious startups to discuss topical issues relevant to change and innovation in the industry. In the past year we've got together over great food and wine to discuss questions like: *What are the opportunities and challenges of APIs? Should innovation happen in a separate location or in HQ? Should corporates partner with startups and how best to do it: invest or incubate?*

If you would like to attend a future Curious Dinner then drop us a line at:

events@adaptivelab.com

### Follow our Flipboard magazine: Bye Bye Banks?

If you're interested in further reading around the topic of banking disruption then you may also be interested in our *Bye Bye Banks?* Flipboard magazine. You will find up-to-date articles covering the latest news relating to the new entrants as well as updates from the established players.

You can follow it here:

http://bit.ly/byebyebanksflipboard

### Subscribe to our regular newsletter: Wunderkammer

Wunderkammer is a fortnightly newsletter, curated by the Adaptive Lab team, that brings together the best content from the prior two weeks covering topics including strategy and innovation, design and technology. Expect articles from the likes of Harvard Business Review, Bloomberg BusinessWeek, TechCrunch as well as independent blogs. The newsletter covers a range of sectors including financial services, healthcare, media, telco - a great way to get a rounded mix of inspiration and insight.

You can sign up to Wunderkammer at:

http://bit.ly/wunderkammernewsletter